AMAZING ENGINE™

System

BUGHUNTERS™

Game

by

Lester Smith

Credits

Designed by Lester Smith

Additional design work by Tim Brown (Chapter 4), Karen Boomgarden and Newton Ewell (Chapter 5), Tim Beach (Chapter 6), and Colin McComb of the clan McComb (Chapter 7 and Starcharts)

Edited by John D. Rateliff

Original AMAZING ENGINE™ design by Zeb Cook

Product Management by Karen Boomgarden

Cover Art by Denis Beauvais

Interior Art by Grant Goleash

Star Map by John Knecht

Cartography by John Knecht

Typography by Angelika Lokotz

Star Map inspired by the stellar grid chart in the *Universe* game by John H. Butterfield, © 1981 SPI.

With thanks to playtesters Ted Carlock, John Davey, Scott Haney, Scott Hutson, John Langford, Steve Taylor, Ron Thrasher, and Andy Turner of the Adventureland Game Club; to Bill Cape, Dave Kinsinger, Sue Kinsinger, Paul Oaks, Jami Riston, Sean Webb, and Sue Wheeler of the Tricounty Gamer Association; and to Michele Carter, Dale Donavan, Colin McComb, Jon Pickens, and Stephen Schend of TSR. Special thanks to W. W. Connors for assistance on stellar distances.

Voyager 1 photographs of Saturn's moons on the Star Map courtesy of NASA.

To Jenny, who said, "That's nice, dear; kill a bug for me."

TSR, Inc
P. O. Box 756
Lake Geneva
WI 53147
U.S.A.

TSR Ltd.
120 Church End
Cherry Hinton
Cambridge, CB1 3LB
United Kingdom

Table of Contents

Introduction:
The BUGHUNTERS™ Universe

Introduction:
The BUGHUNTERS™ Universe

"Do you know why people hate rats and roaches? It's a sort of professional competition. The three toughest creatures in existence, the three species that survive even in the wreckage of a holocaust, are cockroaches, rats, and humans. And we 'synners' are the toughest and most despised of them all."

—Drill Sergeant Andros Owens,
Synthetic Human,
United Terra Reconnaissance and
Peacekeeping Force (UTRPF)

Overview

The BUGHUNTERS™ game is a role-playing simulation of action adventure in a gritty, not-too-distant future. It is a time in which humanity has begun to colonize the worlds of other stars, but the race has at best a tenuous hold on those worlds and is beset by many dangers. The environments of the colony worlds are often hostile, and colonial resources are limited. But what's worse, a host of inimicable aliens prey upon the colonies and have even begun to threaten the safety of Earth itself.

Player characters in the BUGHUNTERS game are "synthetic humans": vat-grown clones of human volunteers, specially modified to serve as starship crews, combat teams, and general troubleshooters for the human race. As members of the United Terra Reconnaissance and Peacekeeping Force (UTRPF), these "synths," or "synners," are often all that stands between the human race and extinction at the hands of a cold and hostile universe.

Synths are tougher than normal humans in many ways. Physically, they have been enhanced to react more quickly, to keep moving longer, and to endure more punishment during battle. Mentally, they are able to withstand the psychological stresses of hyperspace travel, a situation that disorients normal humans, sometimes to the point of madness. Psychically, they have been trained to bear up under the stresses of combat, whether it be against human terrorists or hide-ous, unknown aliens. And they are supplied with the best equipment that human technological ingenuity has to offer. As members of UTRPF ("utter-puff" in synner slang), synners are the unsung heroes of the human race, a buffer from its enemies without, protectors from its enemies within. But for all of that, they are still individuals with hopes and dreams of their own, struggling as much as anyone else to make something of their lives.

The AMAZING ENGINE™ Rules

As part of the AMAZING ENGINE line of role-playing games, the BUGHUNTERS rules build upon the core rules in the AMAZING ENGINE game *System Guide*. **A copy of the AMAZING ENGINE game *System Guide* is required to play the BUGHUNTERS game.**

If you have never created an AMAZING ENGINE character before, the *System Guide* tells both how to generate attributes for your first AMAZING ENGINE character and how to create your Player Core from that character's attributes. The *System Guide* also explains the basics of skill checks, combat, and improving characters through experience—terminology and concepts important to the BUGHUNTERS game.

Of course, if you have already generated a character in one of the other AMAZING ENGINE game universes, you are ready to proceed with the creation of that character's BUGHUNTERS universe incarnation. But first you'll need to know something of the universe in which your BUGHUNTERS game character will be adventuring. The following timeline provides a quick overview of the most significant historical events that have made the expanding demesne of humanity what it is in the BUGHUNTERS milieu.

Introduction:
The BUGHUNTERS™ Universe

A Brief Timeline: AD 2009-AD 2130

AD 2009: Under mounting pressure from numerous multinational corporations and business conglomerates, the United Nations establishes within itself a new voting body, the Economic Assembly, an international business congress of megacorporate representatives, thereby giving these businesses a direct vote on world issues. One of the first motions passed under this new arrangement is to change the name of the United Nations to United Terra, reflecting the newly reached balance of power.

2021: As part of a renewed US push into space, NASA launches the core module of Clarke Station, establishing a long-term space facility in near-Earth orbit.

2039: The Ryan Shield, a practical electromagnetic field generator capable of diverting the hazardous background radiation of space, is developed under the direction of Dr. Avery Ryan at MIT, thereby increasing the feasibility of extended habitation outside the Earth's protective atmosphere.

2043: NASA and the European Space Agency (ESA) pool their resources under a United Terra program, forming the new United Terra Space Association (UTSA). Using Clarke Station as a launching point, UTSA creates Unity Station, a permanent facility on Luna intended largely as a base for construction of future orbital facilities.

2047: Edison Point, a UTSA pure-research lab, is constructed at L-4 from parts prefabricated on Luna.

2056: UTSA starts Bradbury Colony, near the center of Mare Acidalium on Mars. Plans are laid for Burroughs and Wells Colonies at nearby locations, and a long-term terraforming project is begun, largely involving the dropping of ice asteroids onto the planet's far side.

2061: The Isler Jump Drive (named after its chief inventor, Dr. Christine Isler) is developed at Edison Point. Based upon hyperspace experiments originally performed on Earth, the proce-dure proves to operate *much* more effectively at a distance from planetary masses. As a result, the entire Edison Point facility is transported near-instantaneously a distance of some 100,000 kilometers from L-4. When rescued by a shuttle from Luna, lab members complain of lingering disorientation and nausea.

2063: Continued UTSA experimentation to develop an Isler Drive spacecraft yields an engine capable of cycling a vessel through a rapid series of successive jumps. Testing also demonstrates that sleeping occupants of such a vessel suffer less severe malaise. Work proceeds on developing vessels to explore the outer planets of the Solar System.

2066: As a navigational experiment, the Edison Point facility is cautiously returned to L-4 in 1,000-kilometer Isler Drive jumps.

2078: A small Isler Drive spacecraft reaches Jupiter. Travel time is mere days, which the crew spends in drugged sleep. When the ship returns, UTSA initiates a program to develop star travel, hoping to relieve severe population pressures on Earth by colonizing extra-solar worlds.

2079: Scientists at Edison Point create a weak, short-lived, and microscopic—but nonetheless measurable—artificial gravity field.

2081: In a gesture of confidence or hope, UTSA begins construction of Stargate, a launching facility for future starships, at L-5.

2083: An automated probe is sent from Stargate to Alpha Centauri. The round trip takes 13 months, but when the probe returns, it bears proof of a planetary system existing around that star. The second planet out from the twin suns is Earth-like, its breathable atmosphere and warm climate supporting savannahs and lush jungles.

2092: In search of a means of life-support for unconscious starship crew members during the extended times necessary for stellar travel, researchers on Luna devise a stasis field pod. By slowing molecular movement within its field to a virtual halt, such a pod effectively brings time to a near-standstill for its occupant. The new technology also promises a revolution in food indus-

Introduction:
The BUGHUNTERS™ Universe

tries on Earth, allowing for perfect long-term storage of comestibles.

2111: An automated starship with a stasised crew is sent to Alpha Centauri and returns with detailed reports of that system's suitability for human habitation. Plans are begun for establishing an outpost on the system's second world and for eventual wide-spread colonization.

2115: A second vessel is sent to "Acey-Two" (AC-2, Alpha Centauri's second planet) with volunteers for a permanent outpost. Automated probes are sent to Barnard's Star, Wolf 359, Lalande, Sirius, Innes' Star, and UV Ceti.

2117: Staff and materials for a mining outpost are sent to Barnard's Star. Automated probes are sent to Ross 154, Ross 248, and Epsilon Eridani. A breakthrough in genetic cloning research makes it possible to clone mammals; the morality of doing so becomes a hotly debated issue.

2119: An outpost team is sent to Wolf 359. Automated probes are sent to Ross 128 and Groombridge 34.

2120: An outpost team is sent to UV Ceti. Automated probes are sent to 61 Cygni, LFT 1729, and Procyon.

2121: Outpost teams are sent to Ross 154 and Ross 248.

2122: Automated probes are sent to Struve, Epsilon Indi, and Tau Ceti.

2123: An automated cargo ship sent to the UV Ceti outpost fails to return, as does the automated probe sent to Procyon in 2120. A modified probe is sent to UV Ceti to scout out the situation. Experiments with specially modified clones of apes and rats develop an animal largely unaffected by hyperspace jumps.

2125: The UV Ceti probe returns with photos from orbit, showing the cargo ship landed at the outpost but with recordings of radio silence from the facility. A manned mission is launched to investigate the outpost's status.

2127: A single member of the UV Ceti reconnaissance mission returns with a horrifying story of the team's slaughter at the hands of hostile alien creatures.

2128: A cargo ship sent to Ross 154 fails to return. The UT Security Council authorizes secret work to create human clones capable of remaining conscious during hyperspace jumps without subsequent deleterious effects.

2129: A cargo ship sent to Ross 248 fails to return.

2130: The UT Security Council formally announces the formation of UTRPF, a paramilitary force composed largely of clone warriors assigned to protect Earth and its colonies from invasion.

Mission Statement

From the introduction to the UTRPF Soldier's Handbook of Common Tasks:

"UTRPF was established as an elite paramilitary force dedicated to the preservation of human life and human endeavor. As members of its cadre, we have the unique privilege and responsibility of protecting humanity from its enemies on Earth and in space. To a large extent, the future of the race depends upon our performance. If we are strong, brave, dedicated, and honorable, humanity will prosper as its pioneers explore new stars, establish outposts, found colonies, and tame new worlds. But if we are weak, the human race will suffer, its enemies will prosper, and its heirs will languish on Earth, cheated of their birthright.

All the knowledge of the human race is at our disposal. We enjoy the most advanced equipment, the most expert Intelligence, the experience of all human history, and the toughest, best trained soldiers in existence. Together, we stand as humanity's mighty shield, and we strike as the race's terrible sword of Justice. You play an essential part within that proud association, trooper."

Introduction:
The BUGHUNTERS™ Universe

How to Use This Book

Novice Roleplayers: If you are fairly new to role-playing, we suggest that you read through this book pretty much as you would any other: that is, begin at the front and progress toward the back. The contents have purposely been laid out in a progression from most basic information for players to the very deepest knowledge for the Game Master.

Keep in mind, however, that you don't have to read the entirety of this book in order to play the game, and you certainly don't have to commit it all to memory. This isn't a book of law. Rather, the material herein serves as a foundation upon which you and your friends build your adventures. Exactly how you use that material, and where it ultimately takes you, is subject to your imagination.

Experienced Roleplayers: If you are an experienced roleplayer, you are probably in the habit of treating role-playing game rulebooks as reference works, reading them piecemeal, jumping from chapter to chapter in whatever order strikes your fancy and is appropriate to the needs of the moment. That's fine; there is no need for you to read absolutely everything in this book before you begin playing. However, we do suggest that you at least browse through all the sections at some time, to catch the bits of background and atmospheric material scattered throughout. Rather than present all of the material in one long essay, we have divided it up and let it serve as introductions to the appropriate rules sections.

Player's and Game Master's Sections: For simplicity's sake, the information in this book has been divided into two main areas: the first (Part One) for players, and the second (Part Two) for the Game Master. The Players' Section contains information concerning player character creation, skill use, combat procedure, equipment, and humanity's knowledge of the galaxy. The GM's section explains secrets of the milieu (things humanity is not yet aware of and that the player characters should only discover through play) and discusses other game master topics such as awarding experience points and effectively running non-player characters.

GMs should, of course, familiarize themselves with the material in the Players' Section, as well as that in the Game Master's Section.

Players are advised to avoid reading the Game Master's Section, at least at first, so as to have the enjoyment of learning during play the secrets contained therein. If you do read the GM's material, remember that while you, the player, may know this information, your *character* does not share that knowledge and can only learn it from experience. Above all it is strongly recommended that players not read Chapter 10: Sample Adventures, so that the GM may use to fullest advantage the scenarios it contains.

Chapter 1: Character Generation

"I was working in a factory—I say 'I,' because that's how it seems—and I wasn't really satisfied. It wasn't so bad a job: the pay and benefits were pretty good, and you just about had to 'moon' the CEO to get fired. But the work was less than absorbing; and I had this constant, low-level tension that I might lose a finger, or hand, or something. What was worse, though, was that I'd watch these old guys retire and not know what to do with themselves. Most of them would go home and die of uselessness within six months to a year. I didn't want that to be me.

"So when I saw the ad asking for clone donors for United Terra's peacekeepers, I signed up. I remember thinking that I'd have a little extra money coming in that way, and at least a version of myself would get some adventure. That seemed worth any risk from the cloning procedure itself.

"Now back in Bayamón, Puerto Rico, 'I' am once again at work in the factory, probably dreaming of my exploits among the stars. Meanwhile, here I am slogging through a swamp on Acey-Two with a 15-kilo pack on my back, looking for monsters (and not really wanting to find them). I don't know whether to curse 'me' or bless 'me.' But one thing's for certain: there ain't no getting outa this job."

—PFC. Rudy Talavera, UTRPF

The Nature of Synners

Synthetic humans (often referred to interchangeably as clones, synths, or synners) occupy a unique niche in human society. By definition, all synthetic humans serve as members of UTRPF; none are created for any other purpose. By UT law, it is illegal for any body other than UTRPF to create them, and the United Terra Security Council keeps a careful secret of cloning technology, just as the 20th century UN Security Council worked to keep secret the technology and materials used for building nuclear explosives.

Many civil rights activists decry the plight of synthetic humans, insisting that synths are as human as anyone else and that locking them into an occupation as soldiers for UTRPF is tantamount to slavery. And it is undeniable that synths *are* locked into service with UTRPF. Soldiers in normal military organizations sign up for a specific term of service, and once that time has passed they are discharged from further duties, unless they "re-up" (re-enlist) or unless an emergency of some sort allows their government to retain them for the duration of that problem. Furthermore, in most services, normal soldiers can "wash out" during training, being returned to the civilian sector after receiving a less-than-honorable discharge for one reason or another.

Synthetic soldiers of UTRPF do not have these options. Technically, their tour of duty extends until they are no longer needed as protectors of the human race, but no one expects the crisis to end within the foreseeable future. And, in any event, there are no contingencies for their returning to civilian life if it did. Furthermore, synths who wash out of UTRPF training are automatically sentenced to serve as laborers on one of the less-hospitable extra-solar mining outposts. Effectively, then, synthetic humans are UTRPF soldiers now and forever.

Of course, the fact that these clones are physically enhanced to become something more than human means that the average citizen of Earth doesn't really want them to return anyway. As much as the civil rights activists might complain, most people view synths as unnatural and inhuman and fear them accordingly. Often, there is mixed with this fear a tinge of "sour grapes": jealousy due to the fact that UTRPF troopers live a life of excitement and adventure, traveling among the stars.

The Synner's Look

The problem is that as biological clones of normal human beings, synners *look* like normal human beings, albeit unusually well-muscled

Chapter 1: Character Generation

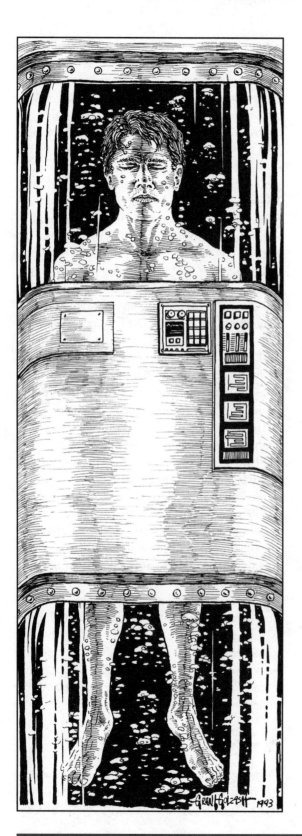

ones. Basically, synthetic humans appear to be young, strong versions of their donors. Regardless of donor age, a synner begins life in a stage of development appropriate to the late teens or early twenties. Players may of course choose to have their PCs be somewhat older than this to reflect time spent gaining rank, skills, and experience.

Force-grown in artificial wombs, developing synths are fed nutrients via their umbilical cord throughout the process, so after "decanting" (the term used for bringing a clone to consciousness and out of the vat) they have navels, just as normal humans do. During their time in the vat, synths' minds are empty, kept in a state of dreamless sleep by electrical control, which also serves to stimulate muscle development, enhanced by chemical treatments through the umbilical. This chemical treatment is also designed to increase bone density and promote organ and skin toughness. Toward the end of the growing process, a special biocompatible plastic is injected in various locations of each synth's body, to further cushion vital organs and supplement the skeleton.

Finally, to clearly identify them as synthetic humans in order to make it difficult for them to hide in normal human society should they choose to go AWOL from UTRPF, synners are given an indelible mark upon their foreheads. This mark (invisible except under black light) is a stylized representation of the Earth and its moon, roughly five centimeters in diameter.

Just prior to decanting, synths receive the mental recording of their donors' personality and memories. On occasion (as explained later), this recording is less than complete, and such synths will have amnesic gaps in their memories. But most receive a full recording and feel as if they *were* the original personality, rather than a clone.

Generating Your Character

To create a BUGHUNTERS™ game player character, simply perform the steps listed in the box below. Each step is fully explained in the

Chapter 1: Character Generation

following pages. Information on how to create normal humans in the BUGHUNTERS™ game milieu is included as well to help the GM create NPCs for the characters to interact with.

One thing to keep in mind as you generate your character is that all BUGHUNTERS game PCs will get plenty of opportunities to combat aliens over the course of a campaign, and all are trained to do so, whatever their specialty. Don't feel obligated to create a combat expert; UTRPF needs synth pilots, and radio operators, and even cooks, as well.

Character Creation Sequence

1. Generate Attributes
2. Calculate Stamina and Body Points
3. Determine Background Occupation
4. List Basic Training Skills
5. Select a Military Service Occupation (MSO)
6. Choose Starting Skills
7. Determine Rank
8. Determine Finances

---

1. Generate Attributes

a) Generate base values for each of your character's attributes, as explained on pages 4-6 of the AMAZING ENGINE™ game *System Guide*. If you are using your character core to generate a character for the BUGHUNTERS universe, follow the examples on pages 6-8 of the *System Guide*.

b) Player characters—and all other synthetic humans in the BUGHUNTERS game— receive a bonus of 30 points to each Physique, Intellect, and Spirit attribute, and 20 points to each Influence attribute. This reflects in game terms the fact that the milieu is a dangerous one. Synthetic humans have been physically, mentally, and emotionally trained and enhanced to account for that fact. Normal humans in the game receive

Chapter 1: Character Generation

a bonus of only 20 points to each of their attributes. It is important to note, for purposes of determining what benefits PC synners derive from their NPC donors, that a donor's Psyche score is thus 10 points *lower* than that of the PC.

2. Calculate Stamina and Body Points

Stamina points for player characters—and all other synthetic humans—in the BUGHUNTERS™ game equal 1/3 the total of Willpower plus Reflexes (rounded up). Body points for player characters—and all other synthetic humans—equal 1/3 the Fitness attribute (also rounded up).

Stamina points for normal human NPCs in the BUGHUNTERS game equal 1/4 the sum of Willpower and Reflexes; body points equal 1/4 the Fitness attribute. It can be readily seen that as synthetic humans, player characters are considerably tougher than normal humans in this milieu, both because of a higher attribute bonus and a more beneficial divisor for stamina points and body points. These advantages are balanced in role-playing terms by the social disadvantages suffered by all synners.

3. Determine Background Occupation

As synthetic humans, BUGHUNTERS game characters are modified clones of normal humans who have donated genetic material and recordings of their brain structure and activity for the purpose. The recording process is neither foolproof nor entirely safe: occasionally a donor suffers brain damage or even dies as a result of the procedure. It is for this reason that only volunteers are used, but more than enough people proffer themselves as subjects to satisfy UTRPF's needs.

Some do it for the money: all donors receive a modest pension for as long as their clone remains in service. Others—particularly the wealthy and/or elderly—do it for the chance at a sort of immortality, hoping that their clone will prove

wily enough to live on long after they are gone.

Besides giving your character borrowed memories of a prior life, the mental recording may also provide some significant skills and other advantages based upon your donor's social status, as detailed below. It is important to note that the skill pools listed beneath each donor class description below increase the **range**, not the **number**, of skills a starting character has to choose among; the actual number of skills known is still dependent on the PC's Learning and Intuition scores (see page 23).

To determine the social status of your character's donor, roll percentile dice, add your character's Position attribute, and find the total on the Donor Background Table. This table can also be used by the GM for generating random NPCs.

Donor Background Table

Donor Social Status	d% + PC Pos*
A. Billionaire	100+[4]
B. Government Leader Corporate Head Millionaire	100+[3]
C. Government Official Corporate Executive Wealthy	100+[2]
D. Military Officer	99-100+
E. Specialist	95-98
F. Teacher	91-94
G. Enlisted Military	80-90
H. Office Clerk	72-79
I. Factory Worker	64-71
J. Sales Clerk	56-63
K. Unemployed Underemployed	1-55

*The superscript numbers mean that for a PC's donor to be of this status, the player must have a modified score of 100 or higher that many times consecutively on the roll for donor background.

Chapter 1:
Character Generation

Remember that the process used to record a donor's mind for duplication in a clone is moderately dangerous. To simulate this, once your donor background has been determined, double the donor's Psyche (which is 10 points below your PC's Psyche): the result is the Transfer Success rating. Make a roll versus this score to see whether or not the mental transcription was performed without trouble. If this roll is less than or equal to the Transfer Success rating, the donor goes through the recording process without a hitch, and your character receives all the listed benefits for that donor's social class. However, if the roll is greater than the Transfer Success rating, the recording is patchy, and the amount by which the roll was failed becomes the percentage chance that each listed skill (and attribute, in the case of the underemployed or unemployed) benefit is lost, *and* that the donor suffers brain damage from the recording process. Donors who suffer such brain damage lose points from Intuition, Learning, Psyche, *and* Willpower equal to the amount by which the brain damage check was missed. Even worse, they have a chance to die from the shock equal to the amount by which the brain damage check failed.

While determining what, if any, benefits PCs derive from their donors, it's a good idea to keep track of all the rolls described in this section on a piece of scratch paper before transferring the results to your PC sheet. The box below contains two examples of donor background generation to illustrate the process.

Donor Background Example

Let's imagine that two players named Baptiste and Linda are generating donor backgrounds for their BUGHUNTERS™ game PCs. Baptiste's PC has a Position rating of 48 and a Psyche of 52, Linda's a Pos of 33 and a Psyche of 46.

Baptiste rolls a 45 on percentile dice which, when added with his PC's Pos of 48, yields a total of 93. This means that his PC's donor

---

falls into a social status of teacher. He next determines the Transfer Success rating by subtracting 10 points from his own Psyche score and doubling the result, for a Transfer Success rating of 84% (52-10=42; 42x2=84). He then rolls versus the Transfer Success rating of 84, and he gets a 36, so he receives all of the listed benefits of the teacher social class without a hitch, and his donor comes through the process safely.

The skill benefits of a teacher background are choices from the Computer, Humanities, Languages, Personality, and Sciences skill pools, so Baptiste can choose his starting skills from any of these pools.

Now it's Linda's turn. Linda rolls a 78 for donor background, which, when added to her PC's Pos of 33, yields a 111, which makes her character's donor at least a military officer. Her total is above 100, entitling her to a second roll. She rolls again and gets an 86, which added to her Pos yields 119, so the donor is now at least social status C. Rolling again, she gets a 75, for a new total of 108, moving the donor to social class B. By now, Linda is very excited. Her next roll is a 71, yielding a total of 104, so her PC's donor is social class A: a billionaire.

She is not so lucky with the Transfer Success check, however. First she determines that her Transfer Success rating is 72% (46-10=36x2= 72). She then rolls a 92, thereby failing the check by 20 (92-72=20). Now she has a 20% chance of losing each of the billionaire donor skill pools and of permanent donor brain damage. She rolls a 49 for the Humanities pool, and a 76 for the Personality pool, so both of them remain okay to choose from. A check for donor brain damage results in an 03, however, so her character's donor suffers a loss of 17 (20-3=17) points to Intuition, Learning, Psyche, and Willpower. Furthermore, there is now a 17% chance that the donor dies from the process. Continuing her sudden run of bad luck, Linda rolls a 13, so her PC's donor is dead.

Chapter 1: Character Generation

A. Billionaire: Such donors are among the wealthiest people in existence. Usually, they are elderly and participate in the program for the sense of immortality to be gained from having a clone live on beyond their own impending deaths.

Billionaire donors are extremely interested in seeing their clones succeed, and they have the wherewithal to help their other selves along. Officially, synners from such donors are no different than any others. But in reality, they have many advantages that most others do not, all related to the fact that their donors are watching over them. For one thing, the personal funds of these synners are effectively unlimited (their bank accounts are always filled with contributions from "an anonymous donor"), allowing them to purchase equipment not normally available and to live in considerable luxury between missions. Also, in case of injury, the absolute best medical care known to humanity becomes available to them as immediately as possible,

often with world-renowned medical experts "volunteering" to aid UTRPF in their care.

Additionally, considerable latitude is typically given to clones of billionaire donors in terms of military discipline. Behavior bordering on insubordination is usually forgiven automatically in their case. There are limits to how far this can be pushed, however, and straightforward disobedience and mutiny are punished as quickly and severely for them as for any other soldier.

PCs whose donors were billionaires can choose starting skills from the Humanities and Personality skill pools in addition to the pools made available by their MSO's (see Step 5 later in this chapter).

B. Government Leader/Corporate Head/Millionaire: Like their wealthier, billionaire-spawned counterparts, clones of major government leaders, international corporate heads, and other millionaires enjoy a large bank account, excellent emergency health care, and considerable latitude in their behavior. The difference is only in degree. Whereas billionaire's clones can buy virtually anything, synners of this slightly lower category must make a Position attribute check to acquire rarer items, with the check modified as the GM sees fit, to reflect relative difficulties.

Like clones of billionaire donors, these synners can choose their starting skills from the Humanities and Personality skill pools. In addition, they may choose from the Computer skill pool.

C. Government Official/Corporate Executive/Wealthy: While these donors do not regularly donate funds to their clones' accounts, they may be able, on occasion, to provide a limited amount of special material for their clones, given enough advance warning to clear the gift through UTRPF headquarters.

Clones of such donors may choose starting skills from the Computer, Humanities, Languages, and Personality skill pools.

D. Military Officer: Many national military and corporate paramilitary officers volunteer as

Chapter 1: Character Generation

UTRPF donors as a means of lending their expertise to humanity's defense in an extra way. Upon occasion, even UTRPF officers volunteer. As explained under Step 7 (Determine Rank) later in this chapter, synners are all enlisted personnel or warrant officers; they are barred from full officer status, which is reserved for normal humans. Of course, in such cases, the clone is assigned to a separate unit from the donor to avoid the potential psychological stress of donors commanding their own clones.

Clones of military officers have the following skill pools available to them from which to choose their starting skills: Basic Training, Military, and Physical Disciplines. Such donors may also serve as an outside source of military gear, at the GM's discretion, and if their clones manage to determine how to contact them.

E. Specialist: The term "Specialist" is used here to mean someone with technical skills, such as a doctor, lawyer, scientist, engineer, architect, computer designer, or the like. Such people typically volunteer as donors for the excitement and pride involved in proving that they could have succeeded in an entirely different sort of life from their own—that of a soldier.

A clone of a specialist donor can have starting skills from the Computer, Engineering, Humanities, Languages, Medicine, Sciences, or Travel skill pools, depending on the exact nature of the donor's specialty. The appropriate skills should be chosen by the player, subject to GM approval; it is the player's responsibility to justify, in terms of donor occupation, the skills chosen.

It is unusual for Specialist donors to have any direct contact with their clones; typically they just read about their exploits once the reports have cleared UTRPF Intelligence. But if direct contact is made, these donors may serve as contacts for specialist knowledge.

F. Teacher: Historically, teaching has been a career that demands considerable knowledge and attention to detail but offers less remuneration than might be expected in terms of both salary and esteem. Nevertheless, teachers continue to arise in every generation. And many 22nd-century teachers share a spark of adventurousness that leads them to volunteer as UTRPF donors.

Clones of these donors may choose starting skills from the Computer, Humanities, Languages, Personality, and Sciences pools; Trivia is a common choice. Additionally, should such donors ever be contacted by their clones, they often serve as eager researchers of information, particularly if it involves scholarly subjects.

G. Enlisted Military: Like military officers, enlisted members of the Earth's various national military and corporate paramilitary forces often volunteer as UTRPF clone donors out of a sense of devotion to protection of the human race. But the pension to be drawn means something to them as well.

Clones of such donors may draw their starting skills from the following pools: Basic Training, Military, and Physical Disciplines. If their clones find some way to contact them (usually surreptitiously, through non-official channels outside UTRPF's attention), these donors may (at the GM's option) serve as a contact for non-standard gear.

H. Office Clerk: This category covers secretaries, file clerks, office receptionists, and suchlike. Those office clerks who become UTRPF donors usually do so out of boredom and dissatisfaction with their lot in life. Spawning an UTRPF clone gives them a vicarious sense of adventurousness, and reports of their clone's actions often restore their faith in themselves. Many times this restored faith, coupled with the financial boost of a pension, empowers such donors to achieve something more with their lives. Frequently, this means a change of career.

Clones of office clerk donors choose their starting skills from the Computer, Humanities, and Personality skill pools.

While it is highly unusual for such donors to be contacted by their clones, it is possible that a synth assigned to a mission on Earth might sometime find such contact useful. In such

Chapter 1:
Character Generation

cases, these donors can serve as a source of inside knowledge in their particular occupation, and they might be willing to house and feed—even hide—their clones. One problem involved with trying to locate these donors, however, concerns the likelihood of their having changed careers since (and because of) becoming an UTRPF donor. Your GM will determine the exact chances of the contact occurring when clones of these donors seek out their originals.

I. Factory Worker: In the 22nd century, by and large, factory workers are factory workers because they like to be. They take some pride in having been trained to do a specific type of labor, and while their wages may be modest, their other benefits (insurance, retirement plan, company input) are usually quite good. In all, the occupation makes for a stable, respectable lifestyle. But occasionally a factory worker will get a hankering to do something out of the ordinary and decides to become a donor for UTRPF. Usually, the sense of adventurousness gained in having done so is sufficient to send the person back to the job, satisfied.

Clones of such donors will have starting skills from the Computer, Engineering, and Humanities skill pools (the actual Engineering skills available may depend on the type of factory the donor worked in).

If, by some chance, factory worker donors are sought out by their clones for assistance, besides possibly providing a place to sleep and eat (and perhaps to hide) they may serve as contacts for such things as construction of specially tooled items, gathering a mob of hard-knuckled friends, and the like (all at the GM's option, of course).

J. Sales Clerk: This category covers everything from auto salespeople to burger shop employees. For many people, retail sales serves as a temporary career while they train for something else. Such donors tend to be young, and the pension they gain from becoming a donor helps them toward their eventual goal (many college students, for example, become donors). However, some are salespeople of fairly expensive

goods such as autos, home electronics, personal computers, and the like, who make good, if sporadic, wages and decide to become a donor either for the regularity of pension checks or the vicarious excitement of "spawning" an UTRPF trooper. Some few other sales clerks are older people, many of them retirees who have returned to work to supplement a retirement pension. For them, becoming a donor yields a bit of discretionary income, and the fact that there is a clone of themselves out and about gives them something of a new lease on life.

Most donors of this category have very little to offer as contacts for their clones, and the younger ones tend to be so mobile as to make it difficult to find them on short notice. If contacted, they can offer little but a place to stay temporarily and, perhaps, a bit of emergency money. Clones of this type of donor may choose starting skills from the Computer, Humanities, and Personality skill pools.

K. Unemployed/Underemployed: The Earth of the 22nd century is a highly urbanized, densely populated place. Automation has "relieved" humanity of the "burden" of most unskilled labor, which means, unfortunately, that holding a job typically requires a great deal more education and/or training than has been the case in the past. And as science makes agriculture, construction, and similar industries more productive, progressively fewer positions are available. The end result is more and more people chasing fewer and fewer jobs, with billions living their lives on welfare or employed in unsatisfactory positions far below their level of expertise.

Unemployed or underemployed donors volunteer typically out of desperation for the pension to be drawn. But they must be quite determined in order to pass the rigorous tests UTRPF imposes for acceptance. To reflect this, clones of such donors add 1d6 to their Willpower attribute. The only starting skills available to PCs with this type of donor are those from the Personality skill pool.

As contacts, these donors are typically of little

Chapter 1:
Character Generation

use to a player character, at the most serving as very poor hosts and possibly as gatherers of other unemployed or underemployed individuals.

4. List Basic Training Skills

During their Basic Training period, all members of UTRPF are trained in a number of basic skills, with particular emphasis on shooting, self defense, and first aid. To reflect this fact, all PCs receive First Aid, Small Arms, and Unarmed Combat as bonus skills *in addition to* those they normally acquire due to their Learning and Intuition attribute (see page 23). A character who already possesses one or more of these three bonus skills (e.g., due to having a Military Officer donor) gains instead a specialization or enhancement of that skill.

5. Select a Military Service Occupation (MSO)

After Basic Training, each member of UTRPF is trained in a specific Military Service Occupation (MSO), ostensibly based upon the individual's natural propensities but actually dependent largely upon UTRPF's needs at the time and the donor's social class.

The MSOs available to synners are listed in the Synthetic Human MSOs table (more mundane MSOs such as Cartographer, Drill Instructor, X-Ray Technician, and the like are reserved for normal humans and are not detailed in this game), in two general divisions: Aerospace and Marines. Each MSO is further identified by prerequisites for entry (if any) and chance of an opening. Donor social status can increase this chance of opening, as shown in the Modifiers for Donor Status subtable.

To select an MSO for a PC, then, first choose one you'd be interested in playing. Make sure your PC's scores meet the prerequisites, then roll percentile dice. If the result is less than or equal to the listed chance of an opening for that MSO (as modified by the donor's social status), then

your PC can sign up for it; otherwise, you must choose a different MSO and roll again. Note that if you ever roll 96-100, UTRPF assigns your character to an MSO for which there is a sudden, special need (i.e., the GM will choose an MSO for your character).

Keep in mind that the MSO your PC begins with does not necessarily dictate the character's permanent assignment. You will have a chance to choose discretionary skills for your PC in the next part of this chapter (Step 6), and you may have your PC switch to a different MSO at some later point; in fact, military services typically encourage such cross training.

A description of each of the MSOs follows, along with the basic equipment usually issued to each in combat situations; this equipment is more fully described in Chapter 5: Equipment.

Chapter I: Character Generation

Synthetic Human MSOs

MSO	% Chance of Opening	Prerequisites
Aerospace:		
Protocol Officer	40%	Cha 60+, Int 40+
Pilot	50%	Lea 55+, Int 45+, Ref 50+
Navigator	55%	Lea 60+, Int 50+
Engineer	60%	Lea 55+, Int 45+, Fit 40+
Doctor	45%	Lea 65+, Int 60+
Cook	55%	Int 55+
Gunner	55%	Ref 60+, Lea 45+
Marines:		
Squad Leader	55%	Cha 50+, Lea 55+, Int 55+
Radio Operator	65%	Lea 50+, Int 40+
Medic	60%	Lea 55+, Int 45+
Scout	60%	Ref 60+, Int 50+
Heavy Weapons Expert	60%	Fit 55+, Lea 40+
Demolitions Expert	55%	Lea 55+, Ref 55+
Grunt	100%	None

Modifiers for Donor Status

Status	Opening Bonus
A	35%
B	25%
C	15%
D	8%
E	4%
F	2%
G	1%
H-K	0%

Example of MSO Generation

After determining their characters' donor backgrounds, Baptiste and Linda proceed to generate initial MSOs for their characters.

Baptiste decides that his character wants to be a pilot. He verifies that his PC has a Lea of 57, an Int of 46, and a Ref of 53—all above the minimum scores listed as prerequisites for that MSO (55, 45, and 50, respectively). There is a base 50% chance of an opening, and the PC's donor social status of F yields a +2% bonus, for a total chance of 52%. Baptiste rolls an 88, so there is no opening available in pilot school; he will have to choose something else. He considers Navigator, but his Lea and Int are too low. So he decides to try for Engineer; his Lea and Int are sufficient, and with a Fit of 48, he is well above the minimum of 40 for that prerequisite. There is a base chance of 60%, plus 2% for donor social class F, for a total chance of 62%. Baptiste rolls a 38 and is accepted into engineer school.

Meanwhile, Linda has been generating her character's MSO as well. She decides that she'd like something that allows high ranks and opts to try for Protocol Officer, noting that her PC's Cha of 66 and Int of 47 satisfy the prerequisites listed for that MSO (60 and 40, respectively). There is a base chance of 40% for her character to be accepted into protocol training, and her donor social status of "A" yields a bonus of 35%, for a total of 75%. Linda rolls a 56, so her character is on the way to becoming a Protocol Officer.

Aerospace MSOs

One of the original reasons for developing synthetic humans was to have them serve as starship crew members. It isn't surprising, then, that UTRPF assigns a great number of its rookie synths to starship crew occupations. The typical niches that these synths are assigned to are detailed here.

Protocol Officer: Protocol Officers are specially trained UTRPF representatives, highly skilled in the arts of diplomacy and thoroughly educated in the details of United Terran law. As such, they serve as mission commanders, as synth team spokespersons in synth/human rela-

Chapter 1: Character Generation

tions, and as official UT arbiters in disputes on humanity's extrasolar worlds and outposts.

Players of Protocol Officer PCs may choose occupational skills from the Humanities, Languages, and Personality skill pools. They *must* choose Protocol (Humanities) and are encouraged to choose Law (Humanities) and Bargaining (Personality).

Basic mission equipment for a Protocol Officer includes a stun pistol and a notepad computer.

Pilot: For UTRPF's purposes, the term "pilot" is used generically to refer to everyone from an ATAPC driver to a starship pilot. Obviously, however, more skill is required to pilot a starship than an ATAPC, and service ranks reflect that fact, as explained later.

Although the military vehicles that BUGHUNTERS™ game PCs will generally be involved with tend to be highly automated, a living mind "behind the wheel" is extremely desirable, and sometimes even crucial—especially in times of combat or other crisis. Consequently, pilots are in high demand in UTRPF's synth forces.

Pilots are typically the ranking officers in charge of their individual mission groups, unless there is a Protocol Officer of at least equal rank present. Even then, command of a pilot's vessel itself is left in the pilot's hands.

Pilot characters may receive skills from the Computer, Engineering, and Travel pools; the Piloting (Travel) skill *must* be one of those chosen for the character. Characters with Surface Piloting only will be assigned to a surface vehicle (typically an ATAPC), those with Aerospace Piloting to an air or interplanetary craft, and those with Hyperspace Piloting to an interstellar starship. Note that a starship may well carry an ATAPC and/or aerospace craft in its hold.

Starting rank for hyperspace pilots is higher than that for aerospace pilots, which in turn is higher than that for pilots of ground vehicles, as explained in the "Determine Rank" section later in this chapter.

Basic mission equipment for a pilot includes a heavy pistol with tracer rounds, a combat knife, a helmet and flak vest, and smartwear.

Navigator: While navigating an auto back and forth to work every day involves no great difficulty, even a simple vacation trip proves the value of having an extra someone to read maps and watch for landmarks. And when it comes to plotting interplanetary or interstellar journeys, a navigator becomes essential.

Like "pilot," the term "navigator" has a very broad usage in UTRPF, referring to anyone from the navigator of a planetary ATAPC or aircraft, to an interplanetary navigator, to a hyperspace navigator. The Navigation skill list in the Travel pool reflects exactly that progression. Navigators are typically second in command to their pilots, third in command if a ranking Protocol Officer is assigned to a mission.

Players of navigator characters may choose skills from the Computer, Engineering, and Travel pools; they *must* choose a Navigation (Travel) skill. Planetary Navigation skill results in the character's assignment to a surface vehicle or aircraft, Space Navigation to an interplanetary craft within a solar system, and Hyperspace Navigation to a starship. Of course, a starship may carry surface, air, or planetary system craft inside.

As with pilots, starting rank is generally higher for navigators with more specialized Navigation subskills.

Basic mission equipment for a navigator includes a heavy pistol with tracer rounds, a combat knife, a helmet and flak vest, smartwear, and a notepad computer.

Engineer: The tools that humans have invented over the ages have grown increasingly more powerful and, by the same token, increasingly more complicated. The more advanced in design they are, the more maintenance they require. Design and maintenance of humanity's tools is the province of engineers, and the sophistication of the equipment UTRPF assigns to its synths makes the engineer character a virtual necessity

Chapter 1: Character Generation

on pretty much any mission team.

Players of engineer characters may choose skills from the Computer, Engineering, and Travel pools, and they *must* choose at least three Engineering skills, two of which must be Electrical Engineering and Mechanical Engineering. Exactly what other Engineering skill or skills are chosen should be based upon the PC's intended arena of expertise. Typically, a single starship will have multiple engineers on staff, each specializing in a different area. Of course, there are some truly expert starship engineers who are as at home with Isler Drives as with computer systems and environmental maintenance, but such talented individuals are few and far between.

Ranks for engineer characters fall within the enlisted range but may rise quite high within it.

Basic mission equipment for an engineer includes an assault rifle, one smoke grenade, one stun grenade, a notepad computer, and a small tool kit; more extensive but less portable tools remain in the ship's utility locker.

Doctor: When an UTRPF mission team is days, months, or even years away from civilization, as is the case during interplanetary or interstellar travel, what might be merely a routine medical problem on Earth can become a life-threatening emergency aboard ship or on an isolated outpost. Consequently, medical personnel are pretty much a necessity for deep-space missions. One fringe benefit of being a ship's doctor is that during combat pretty much everyone on your mission team wants to keep you alive and well at nearly any cost so you'll be able to fix them up afterwards if they need it.

Ship's doctor characters may begin play with skills from the Computer, Humanities, Medicine, and Science pools, and they *must* have the First Aid skill and at least two Medicine specializations.

These characters are always of Warrant Officer Grade, as detailed in the "Determine Rank" section later in this chapter.

Basic mission equipment for a doctor includes a stun pistol, a notepad computer, and a doctor's kit, with more extensive but non-portable medical equipment contained in a ship's sick bay.

Cook: It may seem strange to include this as a PC career in an adventure game, but given the relatively small size of ship crews in the BUGHUNTERS™ milieu, synner cooks perform some very important mission functions. Their primary task, of course, is to prepare meals, but they also serve as quartermasters, keeping a careful inventory of supplies. Most importantly of all, UTRPF trains its cooks to perform as an unofficial morale officer, serving as bartender/psychologist/confessor to the other members of a mission team and working in general to maintain the crew's mental health. A side benefit of being a cook is that the PC's fellow synners will usually try to keep their cook alive if at all possible, rather than face the alternative of computer-generated meals for the long flight home.

Players of cook characters may choose initial skills from the Humanities, Personality, and Sci-

Chapter 1: Character Generation

ences pools; they *must* choose the Cooking (Humanities) skill.

UTRPF cooks typically begin play in the middle of the enlisted ranks.

Basic mission equipment for a cook includes a heavy pistol with tracer rounds, a combat knife, and body armor, as well as a howler machine gun with HEAP (the latter is for use in ship defense and will not normally be carried by cooks assigned to an away team).

Gunner: Ship-to-ship battles don't occur very often in the depths of space, but when they do, an expert with mounted gunnery is a much appreciated member of any ship's crew. Such personnel are also called upon when a particular mission requires the emplacement of stationary and/or automated guns off-ship. And when they are not occupied as mounted-weapons experts, ship's gunners often provide a bit of light maintenance in the Engineering section's aid.

Ship's gunner characters may begin the game with skills from the Engineering, Firearms, and Military pools, and they *must* have the Gunnery (Military) skill.

Generally, these characters begin in the lower enlisted ranks.

Basic mission equipment for a gunner includes an automatic shotgun with flechette rounds, a combat knife, one of each grenade type, and a helmet and flak vest.

Marines:

Throughout history, marines have existed for one main reason: to do battle. That has not changed in the 22nd century; the enemy has just become, if anything, even more dangerous.

Interplanetary vessels are intended to carry a pair of marines at all times as ship's security, and each starship should contain at least a squad of marines, preferably with one or more special troops such as scouts and heavy weapon specialists. However, UTRPF's resources are so overextended by the current crisis that most vessels are lucky to have just one or two marines aboard, forcing the ship's crew to serve double duty as ground troops with the marines simply stiffening the force of that contingent.

Marines are divided into the following MSOs, reflecting the role each plays when enough are present to assemble a squad.

Squad Leader: A specialist in military strategy and tactics (including at least a theoretical knowledge of a wide range of weapons), the UTRPF marine squad leader has the primary responsibility of leading any ground combat operations. Technically, squad leaders are under the command of the ranking officer of the ship that carries their squad, but in practice such officers routinely defer to the squad leader's expertise and give the marines great leeway in achieving mission goals. In those rare situations where multiple squads are assigned to the same ship or facility, they are generally paired into platoons, with the junior squad leader falling under the command of the senior.

Players of squad leader characters may choose skills from the Firearms, Military, and Physical Disciplines pools.

Generally, these characters begin in the upper enlisted ranks.

Basic mission equipment for a squad leader includes an assault rifle, a combat knife, one of each grenade type, and body armor with helmet array and transponder.

Radio Operator: Communications are essential in field operations, whether between squads, with a command post, or with a squad's ship. It is the task of the radio operator to maintain clear, fast communications in even the worst of situations and to do so without compromising the squad's position or the content of those communications. This requires a thorough knowledge of communications equipment and operating procedures, including such things as radio codes and non-electronic signalling techniques (e.g., semaphore). Unfortunately, the value of the radio operator frequently makes this person a prime target if the enemy is capable of recognizing the radio operator's function and importance.

Chapter I:
Character Generation

Radio Operator characters may begin play with skills from the Firearms, Military, and Physical Disciplines pools; they *must* have both the Comm Gear (Military) skill and the Comm Procedure (Military) specialization.

Typically, these characters rank in the lower to middle enlisted range.

Basic mission equipment for a radio operator includes a heavy pistol with HEJA rounds, a combat knife, body armor with helmet array and transponder, and a combat radio.

Medic: Given a well-stocked sick bay, ship's doctors are capable of handling most medical emergencies. But in ground combat operations, someone has to be on the spot to deliver first aid to casualties and stabilize them for transportation back to those facilities. That's the job of a marine squad's medic. When not in combat operations, medics serve as assistants to their ship's doctor, thereby honing their medical skills.

During character creation, medics can receive skills from the Firearms, Medicine, and Physical Disciplines pools; they *must* have First Aid (Medicine) skill.

Beginning medic characters generally fall into the lower specialist ranks.

Basic mission equipment for a medic includes an assault rifle, a combat knife, body armor with helmet array and transponder, and a medkit.

Scout: Although marine squads in general are small and trained to take advantage of cover and concealment during field operations, scouts are true experts in the subjects of infiltration and observation. Often, they are sent individually or in pairs to size up a situation before an entire squad is sent in, in order that the best possible deployment plans can be made.

Players of scout characters may choose skills from the Covert Actions, Firearms, and Physical Disciplines pools for their characters. They *must* choose the Stealth (Covert Actions) skill.

Scout characters typically begin in the lower enlisted ranks.

Basic mission equipment for a scout includes a laser sniper rifle, a heavy pistol with splatter rounds, a combat knife, four smoke grenades, and body armor with helmet array and transponder.

Heavy Weapons Expert: All UTRPF marines receive at least a modicum of training in a wide range of weaponry, from firearms to grenade launchers to flame throwers. What sets the heavy weapons expert apart is intensive training in heavier, more specialized weapons, including mortars, automated machine guns, and beam generators. One notable result of this training is that heavy weapons experts tend to find themselves assigned to the deadliest missions, because that is where they are most needed.

Players of heavy weapons experts may choose skills from the Firearms, Military, and Physical Disciplines pools. They *must* choose Heavy Weapons (Firearms) as a skill.

These characters begin play in the specialist ranks, generally toward the middle of the scale.

Basic mission equipment for a heavy weapons expert includes a heavy pistol with HEJA rounds, a combat knife, a grenade launcher with six rounds of each grenade type, a flame thrower, and body armor with helmet array and transponder.

Demolitions Expert: UTRPF troops have a wide range of weapons available to them, from hand guns to flame throwers and mortars. But for some jobs, that just isn't enough. Whether it's breaching a reinforced wall, removing several tons of earth, or obliterating a nest of nasty xenoforms, whenever a really big hole has to be made in a hurry, demolitions is often the best answer. And of course, with that much destructive power at hand, an expert at its use is advisable.

Demolitions Expert characters may receive skills from the Firearms, Military, and Physical Disciplines pools. They *must* choose the Demolitions (Military) skill.

These characters typically begin play in the lower to middle specialist ranks.

Basic mission equipment for a demolitions expert includes an assault rifle, a combat knife,

Chapter 1: Character Generation

one of each grenade type, six satchel charges, a notepad computer, and body armor with helmet array and transponder.

Grunt: Of course, the bulk of most marine squads consists of simple foot soldiers. Consequently, this is the one MSO that is always in need of new members and into which new recruits can count on being accepted if they lack the prerequisites for any other MSOs, or if those MSOs are temporarily filled.

Grunt characters can begin play with skills from the Firearms, Personality, and Physical Disciplines pools. There is no particular skill that they *must* choose, but often they devote themselves to expertise with one or more particular firearms and/or melee combat skills.

These characters begin the game in the lowest of the enlisted ranks.

Basic mission equipment for a grunt includes an assault rifle with grenade launcher, three launchable frag grenades, two launchable stun grenades, one launchable incendiary grenade, one of each hand grenade type, a combat knife, and body armor with helmet array and transponder.

6. Choose Starting Skills

After determining your PC's profession, or MSO, it is time to choose starting skills. Professional skills are equal to one-tenth of the character's Learning score, rounded up, and can be chosen from those skill pools made available by both donor level and MSO. **Be careful to include in your pick any skills listed as "musts" in your PC's MSO description.** In addition, you may choose discretionary skills from any and all pools, one for every 15 points of the character's Intuition (rounded down).

A Note on Languages: In the 22nd century of the BUGHUNTERS™ milieu, English continues to be the dominant language in world events. Because of this, even clones of non-English-speaking donors know English due to its inclusion in the mental recording they receive just prior to "decanting" (in other words, all BUGHUNTERS game PCs speak English).

But other languages are certainly spoken, and skill in one or more of them may come in handy during adventures, whether on Earth or off, as PCs interact with colonists, L-5 workers, and others, human and synner alike. For that reason, players may decide to choose additional languages for their characters, assigning them as skills. It's up to the player to decide whether such an extra language is the donor's native tongue or one the donor or synner picked up later on in life. A list of the most common languages, those with the greatest number of native speakers, is included in the skill descriptions in the next chapter.

Skill Specialties and Enhancements: In the BUGHUNTERS game, specialty and enhancement skills (as explained on pages 12-13 of the *System Guide*) generally apply to particular types of equipment or a specific area within a larger field. The purpose of the enhancement rule is to allow players to give their characters true expertise when firing a particular type of pistol, piloting a specific kind of vehicle, or attempting to answer a question within a specific field. Rather than extend the skill list needlessly with reams of examples, we list samples where appropriate in the skill descriptions in the next chapter, leaving it to the individual players to suggest appropriate enhancements for their characters and to individual GMs to approve or deny those requests as seems fitting.

Chapter I:
Character Generation

Skill List (by pools)

BASIC TRAINING

All PC synths who have undergone Basic Training gain the three following bonus skills: First Aid (Medicine), Small Arms (Firearms), and Unarmed Combat (Physical Disciplines).

COMPUTER
Computer Systems (Int)
      Computer Programming (Lea)

COVERT ACTIONS
Camouflage (Int)
Disguise (Cha)
Lockpicking, Mechanical (Ref)
Searching (Int)
Security Systems (Lea)
      Lockpicking, Electronic (Lea)
Stealth (Ref)
Survival (Lea)

ENGINEERING
Engineering, Electrical (Int)
      Electronic (Lea)
            Computer (Lea)
            Isler Drive (Lea)
            Stasis Field (Lea)
Engineering, Mechanical (Int)
        Firearm Maintenance (Lea)
        Power Plant (Lea)
            Nuclear (Lea)
            [requires Electronic & Physics]
        Vehicle Maintenance (Lea)
            Aircraft (Lea)
            Spacecraft (Lea)
            Surface Craft (Lea)
Engineering, Environmental (Lea) [requires Electronic, Mechanical, and Biology]

FIREARMS
Small Arms (Ref)
      Sidearms (Ref)
      Longarms (Ref)
Heavy Weapons (Ref)
      Anti-Armor Weapons (Fit)
      Grenade Launchers (Fit)
      Mortars (Int)
Autofire (Fit)

HUMANITIES
Art (Int)
Bureaucracy (Int)
Cooking (Int)
History (Lea)
Law (Lea)
Linguistics (Lea)
Literature (Int)
      Writing (Cha)
Music (Int)
      Instrument (Cha)
Philosophy (Lea)
Protocol (Int)
Religion (Lea)
Sports (Lea)
Xenological Theory (Int)

LANGUAGES

All languages are Int skills.

MEDICINE
First Aid (Int)
General Medicine (Lea)
      Emergency Medicine (Lea)
      Psychiatry (Lea) [requires Psychology]
      Stasis Medicine (Lea)
      Surgery (Lea)
      Synthetic Medicine (Lea)

MILITARY
Comm Gear (Int)
      Comm Procedure (Lea)
      Isler Radio (Lea)
Demolitions (Lea)
Environmental Suit (Int)
Gunnery (Int)
Leadership (Cha)
Military Science (Lea)

PERSONALITY
Bluffing (Cha)
      Bargaining (Cha)
      Gambling (Cha)
Luck (Psy)
Street Smarts (Cha)
Trivia (Wil)

PHYSICAL DISCIPLINES
Armed Combat (Ref)
Athletics (Ref)
Brawling (Fit)
Climbing (Ref)
Grappling (Ref)
High-G Maneuver (Fit)
Low-G Maneuver (Ref)
Swimming (Fit)
Throwing (Ref)
Unarmed Combat (Ref)

SCIENCES
General Sciences (Int)
      Biology (Lea)
      Chemistry (Lea)
      Physics (Lea)
      Psychology (Lea)

TRAVEL
Navigation, Planetary (Int)
      Navigation, Space (Lea)
            Navigation, Hyperspace (Lea)
Piloting, Surface (Int)
      Piloting, Aerospace (Lea)
            Piloting, Hyperspace (Lea)

Chapter 1:
Character Generation

7. Determine Rank

To the uninitiated, rank and chain of command in UTRPF may seem a bit complicated, but it all becomes clear if a few basic facts are understood.

First, for historical reasons, the *names* for ranks are different between aerospace and marine forces, although they both use the same *rating* structure. That is to say, an E3 (enlisted rate 3) member of the UTRPF marines is paid the same, and bears the same authority, as an aerospace E3, even though the former is called a Private First Class and the latter a Starhand.

Second, the specialized skills demanded by certain MSOs have led to the creation of the Specialist ranks, a short progression of enlisted ranks parallel to the normal series. In terms of chain of command, these specialist ranks are something of an anomaly. In purely military matters, the highest-ranked Specialist (Spec 7) is still subject to command by a E4 Starmate or Lance Corporal, but even higher-ranking members of the normal progression tend to defer to a lower-ranking specialist concerning matters that fall within that specialist's area of expertise. While the wisdom of this dual-line set-up has been questioned often, most authorities agree that the Specialist rank structure is a necessity.

Third, it should be kept in mind that only normal humans are allowed to be commissioned as officers in UTRPF. Humanity wants to keep final command authority firmly in human hands. But the desire to have some sort of officer-like authority in command of a starship even during hyperspace travel—when any normal humans on board are, of necessity, in stasis—has led to the establishment of a line of Warrant Officer ranks parallel to the normal officer ranks. For the sake of easy recognition of rank progression, those warrant officer ranks beyond the first two echo the names of full officer ranks, but with an additional designator—"Star" for aerospace and "Sword" for marines. In effect, then, UTRPF warrant officers serve in the capacity of normal offi-

cers in all cases *except* when human officers are present. As a matter of fact, in practice, the terms "Sword" and "Star" are typically dropped during normal operations, just as the term "Light" is generally ignored unless someone specifically wants to stress at some point the subordination of a Light Lieutenant to a full Lieutenant, or a Light Commander to a full Commander.

PC Starting Rank: In theory, all UTRPF personnel begin their careers at the bottom of the enlisted, warrant officer, or officer (human only) ranks and progress from that point one step at a time, with regular promotions based upon longevity—assuming satisfactory service, of course.

But in practice, some individuals advance in rank much more quickly than do others. Talent at one's MSO has something to do with this, but to a greater extent, the advancement of these individuals is the result of their adeptness at "playing the system." They have an eye for what tests must be taken, what reports must be filed, and whose attention must be drawn in order to gain points toward promotion. Of course, the actual MSO chosen has a great deal to do with a character's rank.

In game terms, then, rank is based upon a character's Pos, with a modifier applied for MSO. The MSO modifiers are listed in the Rank Modifiers table on the next page. To generate a starting rank for your PC, then, add to the character's Pos rating the MSO modifier listed and compare the result to the UTRPF Rank Equivalency table.

Note that, as play progresses, your PC's Pos may increase, due to experience, possibly making the character eligible for a rank increase. Of course, eligibility does not mean automatic increase in rank: promotion can only occur at the official authorization of UTRPF headquarters. In other words, actual reception of that new rank will be subject to your GM's discretion and may be delayed for some time due to campaign considerations.

Chapter 1:
Character Generation

Rank Modifiers

Aerospace MSOs:	Bonus	Maximum		Marine MSOs:	Bonus	Maximum
MSO	Points	Rank		MSO	Points	Rank
Protocol Officer	210	WO6		Squad Leader	200	WO5
Pilot	105/155/205*	WO6		Radio Operator	5	E6
Navigator	100/150/200**	WO5		Medic	10	E7 (Spec. 7)
Engineer	30	E9		Grunt	0	E7
Doctor	200	WO5		Scout	10	E8
Cook	50	E9		Heavy Weapons Expert	15	E7 (Spec. 7)
Gunner	0	E7		Demolitions Expert	15	E7 (Spec. 7)

*The points given are for Surface, Aerospace, & Hyperspace Pilots, respectively

**The points given are for Planetary, Space, and Hyperspace Navigators, respectively

UTRPF Rank Equivalencies

Rank Points	Rating	Aerospace Title	Marine Title	Specialist Title
Enlisted Ranks:				
0	E1	Recruit	Private One	
40	E2	Cadet	Private Two	
55	E3	Starhand	Private First Class	
70	E4	Starmate	Lance Corporal	Specialist Four
85	E5	Petty Officer Three	Sergeant	Specialist Five
100	E6	Petty Officer Two	Staff Sergeant	Specialist Six
115	E7	Petty Officer	Gunnery Sergeant	Specialist Seven
130	E8	Chief Petty Officer	Master Sergeant	
145	E9	Senior Chief Petty Officer	Sergeant Major	
Warrant Officer Ranks:				
230	WO1	Warrant Officer	Warrant Officer	
245	WO2	Chief Warrant Officer	Chief Warrant Officer	
260	WO3	Star Lieutenant	Sword Captain	
275	WO4	Light Star Commander	Sword Major	
290	WO5	Star Commander	Light Sword Colonel	
305	WO6	Star Captain	Sword Colonel	
Officer Ranks:*				
230	O1	Ensign	2nd Lieutenant	
245	O2	Light Lieutenant	1st Lieutenant	
260	O3	Lieutenant	Captain	
275	O4	Light Commander	Major	
290	O5	Commander	Light Colonel	
305	O6	Captain	Colonel	
—	O7	Commodore	Brigadier	
—	O8	Admiral	General	

***All officer ranks are reserved for normal humans and are listed here for purposes of comparison only.

Chapter 1: Character Generation

Example of Rank Determination

Linda and Baptiste now set about determining their characters' starting ranks. Baptiste's PC has a Pos of 48. Engineer yields a rank bonus of 30, so his PC has a rank point total of 78 (48+30), which results in a starting rank of Starmate (Aerospace E4). Linda's PC has a Pos of 33, and Protocol Officer yields a rank bonus of 210, so her PC has a rank point total of 243, sufficient for a rank of Warrant Officer (Aerospace WO1).

8. Determine Finances

Given their situation as perpetual soldiers for UTRPF, synners have little use for personal property. Most pieces of mission equipment—particularly firearms—are owned by the force and, although assigned to particular individuals, are distributed only during actual missions. During the rest of the time, they remain in the armory or supply office. Food and lodging are also supplied by UTRPF, as is entertainment of various sorts.

Discretionary Spending: Nonetheless, a bit of discretionary spending is considered necessary for emotional health, so synths are given a monthly stipend of UTRPF scrip with which to purchase personal items. But in a typically military sort of way, much of this stipend must go toward upkeep of uniforms, and most synths spend a great deal of it paying for alternate housing and food (military barracks and meals growing tiresome after a while).

The amount of stipend available for completely discretionary spending each month is double the PC's rank points, triple if the character does some extreme "belt-tightening." However, each month of penny-pinching temporarily reduces the PC's Pos score by one point. Devoting all of a subsequent month's discretionary income to entertaining will restore the Pos loss.

PCs may spend their discretionary funds however they wish (within reason). What items can-

not be found at the PX (**P**ost **Ex**change store) can sometimes be bought on the black market. UTRPF frowns on synners owning anything that cannot be bought at the PX, but some officers and civilians are willing to trade civilian currencies for UTRPF scrip or sell outside items for it, often at an exorbitant exchange rate. Chapter 5: Equipment lists prices for many items PCs may wish to purchase. GMs may use current, real-world, US prices as a guide for the cost in UTRPF scrip of other items.

Assigned Equipment: Besides their uniforms and MSO manuals, PCs are assumed to have been assigned equipment appropriate to their particular MSO. Normal equipment is listed under each MSO description, but GMs may change this as they wish for specific missions, giving PCs more equipment for tougher-than-usual missions or insisting that they carry lighter weaponry, or even none at all, for more peaceable assignments.

Improving Your Character

Characters in the BUGHUNTERS™ game are not static; they change as a result of their experiences. For PCs to change MSOs, a PC must fulfill the prerequisites for the new MSO and must already possess any skills listed as "musts" in that MSO's description. Such applications can only be made once per month, and only when the PC is at some UTRPF base capable of processing the paperwork (e.g., Stargate). Of course, the PC must still roll to see if there is an opening in the desired MSO.

In addition to changing MSOs, PCs can also buy new skills, improve their attribute scores, and buy additional dice for their Player Core. Attribute scores are increased one point for every five points of experience spent for this purpose. New skills, specialties, and enhancements cost 50 experience points each, while each new die purchased for the Player Core costs 100 experience points.

Chapter 2: Skills

In the BUGHUNTERS™ game, as in all AMAZING ENGINE™ milieus, a character's skills serve as a sort of shorthand notation of what the character is best at, not a limiter of what the character can attempt to do. In other words, as you play the role of your character, don't merely look for chances to use your PC's listed skills—rather, let those skills help you to get into the role of the PC.

The distinction between these two approaches may seem subtle, but it points out what makes role-playing unique from other types of gaming. Most gaming involves using game mechanics—numbers, board position, rules, etc.—to best advantage, so as to *win*. Winning is first and foremost in such games. Not so in role-playing. In RPG sessions, winning is desirable, of course, but it isn't the end-all. In fact, even losing—whether it be undergoing a temporary setback or even suffering death—advances the plot and gives you a chance to act the role of your character.

And acting the part of a character is what role-playing is all about. Whether you are the type of role-player who actually speaks in the voice of your PC or one who describes the PC's actions like a novelist—and most role-players are a mixture of both—you should judge what your character should do in a given situation by what a real person with his or her background might do in a similar situation.

It is important to remember at all times that **PCs can attempt any skill listed on their character sheet** (see page 125 of this book), **except for skills which involve Lea checks**; this reflects their wide-ranging abilities. Characters attempting a skill they do not possess have one-half the chance of success a character with the skill would have. But if you are truly playing a character, you may wish to attempt something that isn't covered by the BUGHUNTERS game skill list. No list of skills can fully reflect all the possibilities of human endeavor, and humans are inventing new technologies—requiring new skills—every day.

That's why role-playing games require a Game Master: to decide how to handle unforeseen situations. And it's why the AMAZING ENGINE game system relates all skills to a few basic attributes, allowing a GM to have you check against one of those attributes and allowing the invention of new skills to reflect the specific needs of individual campaigns.

As you choose and use skills for your PC, then, think of them as making up a skeleton from which to envision the character. Your acting of that character's role will be the PC's flesh and blood, in effect.

Specialties and Enhancements

In the BUGHUNTERS game, the penalty for characters attempting to use a specialty they do not possess is –20 per level between the specialty and its parent skill. The bonus for gaining an enhancement is +10 to the skill level.

Skill Descriptions

The bulk of this chapter is devoted to descriptions of the individual skills in the BUGHUNTERS game. Fuller details of how the various combat and medical skills are used are given in Chapter 4: Combat and Repair; the travel skills are more fully described in Chapter 6: Ships.

The skill descriptions below are arranged alphabetically by skill pool, then by skill within each pool.

Basic Training

This "pool" is merely a convenient catch-all for those three skills belonging to other pools that all UTRPF personnel gain in the course of their basic training: **First Aid**, from the Medicine skill pool; **Small Arms**, from the Firearms skill pool; and **Unarmed Combat**, from the Physical Disciplines skill pool. Each of these skills is described under the appropriate skill pool below.

Chapter 2: Skills

Computer

Computers of the 22nd century are quite sophisticated, but not incredibly different from those of the late 20th century. While the most advanced 22nd-century computers are composed of chemical "hardware," most computers the PCs encounter are still solid state, for durability. Computer systems within the Solar System are all pretty much interconnected (except for special cases, where isolation is desirable for security reasons), allowing the average citizen immediate access to an encyclopedic array of knowledge. However, the radio lag that causes merely annoying access delays between Earth, its orbital facilities, Luna, and the Mars colonies effectively isolates completely the computer systems of traveling starships.

On the other hand, increasing improvements in data storage, memory capacity, and software design have given rise to a number of significant changes even in portable computers. For one thing, the design of machines with multitudinous separate processors capable of operating in parallel or sequentially—depending upon the task at hand—has given rise to more than mere terabytes of RAM; it allows for a measure of sapience, particularly in shipboard mainframes and larger machines. Personality-emulating software assists in presenting such computers as individual beings, making them truly "user-friendly." Data entry is routinely by voice, with electronic stylus and pad for making sketches or jotting notes, particularly in hand-sized portables; keyboards are reserved for inputting large amounts of critical information in a short period of time (since typing is much faster than writing longhand). Data storage is by means of holographic crystals, allowing even the tiniest of computers to hold a wealth of information. On Earth, recyclable paper is still the cheapest, most efficient medium for hard copy; in space, hard copy is typically done on paper-thin plastic sheets with an electromagnetic dot matrix built in, capable of repeated erasure and reuse.

Nor are 22nd-century computers merely involved with information processing. Entertainment in the forms of "trideos" (holographic movies), videos, music, and games are all tied into the personal computer. Users are able to record, play back, modify, compose and otherwise interact with all such materials with incredible freedom.

Computer Systems (Int): Computers are integral to pretty much every occupation in the 22nd century, serving as a ready assistant in nearly every human endeavor, from stellar navigation to cooking or music. Fortunately, voice input and display iconography make them so easy to operate that virtually anyone can puzzle out how to use most models with just a few minutes of tinkering. It is for this reason that the Computer Systems skill has been related to the Intuition attribute.

Computer Programming (Lea): Designing software and/or hardware for specific functions requires a bit more expertise than simple computer operation; hence this specialty. Computer-assisted design programs can make the task somewhat easier, but extensive programming or physical modification of a system still requires a great deal of skill, particularly if the system is hostile to such attempts.

In most cases, the Computer Programming specialty is sufficient for BUGHUNTERS™ adventures. But for players who wish to design true computerphile PCs, the option of expertise in more specific programming languages is provided. For purposes of this game, those languages are divided into two general specialties: *collator* languages and *amassive* languages. It is assumed that an expert in either type is able to deal with pretty much any programming language of that type.

In the BUGHUNTERS game, scientific and military applications tend to use amassive languages; collator languages are of primary use in government and business computer systems.

Chapter 2: Skills

Covert Actions

Under this heading are collected skills of primary use to a scout or other such person dependent upon stealth and infiltration.

Camouflage (Int): Camouflage is the skill at making things blend into their backgrounds. Requiring an eye for hiding things, it covers techniques of both personnel camouflage (clothing and facial makeup) and area camouflage (using artificial or natural foliage to break up the outline of vehicles, tents, and even buildings).

Disguise (Cha): Whereas camouflage attempts to make things invisible to the eye, the disguise skill seeks to make them appear as something other than they are. Of course, making a pile of pillows and blankets appear to be a sleeping figure is much less difficult than making a person appear as someone else, especially if the two individuals in question are different in build or if viewers are well acquainted with one or the other of them. Your GM will set modifiers to the use of this skill as the situation dictates.

Lockpicking, Mechanical (Ref): Electronic locks are common in the 22nd century, especially in high-tech facilities such as the great majority of those off-Terra. In spacecraft, they are virtually universal.

But mechanical locks still have their uses, especially in places where power for electronic locks is not readily available or where cost is a prime consideration. Besides being in use in at least half of the residences on Earth, mechanical locks are also the typical means of securing smaller enclosures such as lockers and chests.

Mechanical Lockpicking skill confers upon its possessor the ability to open such locks with relative ease. Opening mechanical locks with improvised tools is a normal skill roll; specialized tools confer a bonus to your chances, as set by your GM (typically +10 to +20). Persons without this skill gain no bonuses from using lockpicking tools.

Searching (Int): Searching is skill at locating unseen items. Sometimes it merely involves knowing what to look for and the likeliest places to find it (such as when searching a building for a misplaced file folder); at others it means recognizing potential hiding places (such as realizing that a particular shadow is big and dark enough to hide an assailant). By the same token, it yields its user skill in hiding things.

Whenever a character attempts to use this skill, the GM will first make a determination as to whether the hidden item is merely unseen or is purposely hidden. In the first case, penalties to the chance may or may not apply, depending upon the exact situation (size and color of the object, size of area, etc.). But in the latter case, any searchers must subtract from their Searching skill half of the hider's appropriate skill (Camouflage, Stealth, or Searching, depending upon the situation).

Security Systems (Lea): The Security Systems skill represents a familiarity with typical equipment and procedures used to protect a location from thieves, spies, and other less sinister—though no less unwelcome—intruders. Exactly

Chapter 2: Skills

what constitutes a "location" depends upon the situation, but it might range from a single room to an entire complex of buildings.

Upon viewing the location (or the plan of one), persons who succeed at a roll against this skill will recognize the best positions for security cameras and other sensor equipment, for optimum patrol routes, and the like. Likewise, such persons will recognize any relative weaknesses in a security system they view.

Of course, optimum plans are not always feasible to put into practice in a given situation, due to shortages of guards and security equipment, so actual placement of sensors and patrol routs may vary from what the character would identify as best. And it may well be beyond the capability of the character to exploit any relative weaknesses that are perceived.

Lockpicking, Electronic (Lea): Advances in electronic security measures typically remain just one step ahead of developments to bypass those security measures. Characters with the Electronic Lockpicking skill are learned in those developments, knowing the techniques and equipment necessary for bypassing electronic locks and sensors.

While a very few, very simple such devices may be thwarted with improvised tools, or without any tools at all, most require both the right skill and the right equipment, and a few of the most advanced devices remain unthreatened by even the best. The GM will set skill modifiers based upon the exact devices to be thwarted and the exact equipment available to the user of this skill.

Stealth (Ref): Quite simply, this is the skill of moving quietly and secretively, so as not to be seen or heard. The GM will apply skill modifiers based upon light and noise in the user's environment at the time of the stealth attempt and will decide how many skill tests must be made for a particular attempt, based upon how much distance must be covered, how many potential observers are present, and other relevant factors.

Survival (Lea): Most modern people are not very skilled at surviving in the wild. More than one, after being lost in a desert, has been found dead of dehydration with water still in a canteen, for example. On the other hand, survival experts have been able to get by for long periods of time in some of the Earth's harshest climes, surviving on a diet of insects and worms in some cases, and retrieving water from local plants and/or soil.

The Survival skill, then, involves recognizing sources of safe food and water (and possibly air) in a harsh environment, avoiding deadly aspects of that environment, and inuring oneself to hardship so as to ration resources to best effect.

The GM may set skill modifiers and success and/or failure margins for particularly hostile environments. In such cases, great success might mean the retaining of perfect health, simple success might mean survival but with a gradual loss of stamina points, simple failure might mean body point loss, and terrible failure might mean a deadly occurrence of some sort.

Engineering

High technology requires expert maintenance. This is especially critical during voyages through the interstellar wastes, when a vessel is months—or even years—away from Earth. The skills listed in this category are concerned primarily with such maintenance. While characters may use these skills to engineer new devices, most of the time they will be devoting them to just keeping their equipment functioning.

Engineering, Electrical (Int): The Electrical Engineering skill involves a solid knowledge of electrical power and its basic behaviors. Characters with this skill are able to work with, repair, and even design wiring systems (to some extent), so as to supply electrical power where needed in a facility without electrocuting themselves in the process. They are also able to design and repair relatively simple electrical devices involving lighting elements, heating coils, motors, solenoids, and the like.

Electronic (Lea): A deeper knowledge of elec-

Chapter 2: Skills

tricity, Electronic Engineering involves a familiarity with the properties of conductors, capacitors, semiconductors, transducers, printed circuits, and integrated circuits for use in electronic devices from hand-held calculators to shipboard radios.

Computer (Lea): Specialization in Computer Engineering represents a knowledge of the applications of electronics to computer architecture in particular, along with the ability to repair and maintain computers.

Isler Drive (Lea): Isler Drive Engineering involves knowledge of the electronic devices that collectively generate the Isler Drive effect in starships, allowing for repair and maintenance of the engines necessary for hyperspace travel.

Stasis Field (Lea): This specialty represents detailed knowledge of the circuitry of the stasis pods in which normal humans typically spend their time during hyperspace travel, allowing a character with this skill to maintain and, if necessary, repair such pods.

Engineering, Mechanical (Int): The Mechanical Engineering skill can be described most simply as involving things with moving parts. In engineering terms, it concerns the physical properties of materials—including such things as durability, malleability, stress tolerances, friction, etc.—and geometric issues such as lever angles, gear ratios, and the like. In maintenance terms, it simply means keeping machinery working.

Characters with this skill are able to assemble and disassemble machinery. With the right equipment, they can weld metals, machine basic replacement parts, and even make many specialized tools for their work.

Firearm Maintenance (Lea): Firearms are intricate devices which, if not functioning correctly, can be deadly to their users. Specialization in Firearm Maintenance allows a character to keep firearms in perfect working order. It also allows its possessor to safely puzzle out the workings of alien weapons.

Power Plant (Lea): This specialization involves the application of mechanical engineering skills to power plants such as electrical generators and combustion engines. Its possessors are familiar with the special mechanical problems involved in such high speed, high torque applications.

Nuclear (Lea): For maintenance of nuclear plants (fusion and, in some rare cases, fission), a very specialized knowledge is required of nuclear reactions, how to control them, and how to convert the resultant heat energy into usable mechanical or electrical power (usually through steam). *Characters can only acquire this specialty if they already possess specializations in Electronic (Engineering) and Physics (Sciences).*

Vehicle Maintenance (Lea): This specialty is pretty much self-explanatory, simply involving the keeping of vehicles in running condition. Note, however, that its subspecialties are divided somewhat differently than those of the Piloting and Navigation skills in the Travel pool. This reflects the fact that while it is a *much* different task to pilot an interstellar craft than one designed for atmospheric travel, the maintenance tasks are not that much different (especially given that Isler Drive is a separate skill entirely).

Aircraft (Lea): This specialty relates to maintenance of any vehicle with a motive force that depends upon an atmosphere as its medium.

Spacecraft (Lea): The Spacecraft specialty applies to any vehicle that operates in an off-world vacuum. The specialty may also be of some use in orbital facilities, lunar bases, etc, particularly as relates to the maintaining of hull integrity, artificial gravity, and similar concerns. In terms of hull integrity, it may also be of use with deep-sea facilities and vehicles.

Surface Craft (Lea): This specialty covers the maintenance of ground and water vehicles. It is, by nature, primarily concerned with how their motive power interacts with ground or water; it therefore includes the propulsion of submarines and submersibles.

Engineering, Environmental (Lea): The Environmental Engineering skill concerns the operation and upkeep of atmosphere, temperature,

Chapter 2: Skills

water, food, and gravity in enclosed systems. Primarily, this means spacecraft, space stations, and other bases in terribly hostile environments. But it can also mean deep-sea facilities and long-term submarines. *Characters seeking this skill must first possess the Mechanical Engineering skill as well as a specialty in both Electronic and Biology (Sciences).*

Firearms

The skills under this heading involve the use of various types of human-portable ranged-fire combat weapons, from pistols to mortars. There has not been as much change in firearms over the one hundred and thirty-odd years since the end of the 20th century as some might think; certainly there have been no sweeping adoptions of radical new designs. While a few experimental railguns have been developed in Earth orbit, the success of United Terra and subsequent lack of major combatants has caused a general slowing down in design of major weapons systems.

At the level of personal weapons, the three greatest changes have been that 1) caseless ammunition has become universal, and cartridges a distant memory, 2) computer-assisted targeting has become a reality even on the lightest of hand weapons, and 3) weapon rates of fire have steadily increased. The latter is something of a mixed blessing, allowing for greater coverage of an area with autofire but requiring a trooper to carry much more ammunition into battle.

Lasers are still fairly large, the smallest being the rather-bulky "Deadeye" sniper rifle. Their dependence upon considerable electrical power has limited their use as other than a vehicle weapon; but in space, where maneuvering room, incredible speeds, and lack of a blocking horizon make distances from firer to target much vaster, speed-of-light velocity and pin-point firing precision has made lasers the weapon of choice for vessels.

Autofire is a special case, since it can be used

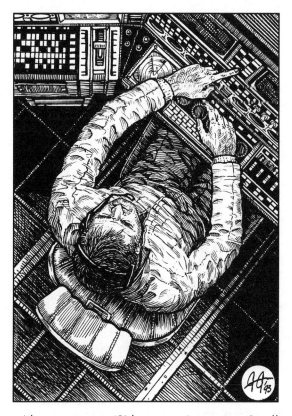

with any weapon (Sidearms or Longarms, Small Arms or Heavy Weapons) capable of fully-automatic fire. Players and GMs should note that, *when these weapons are being used in autofire mode,* such use requires the Autofire skill rather than a normal roll against the skill or specialty for that weapon.

Details of the effects of various firearms during play are given in Chapter 4: Combat & Repair and Chapter 5: Equipment.

Small Arms (Ref): With the Small Arms skill, a character has enough basic knowledge of the workings of any personal firearms to be able to use them in combat, albeit at a skill penalty. Specialization in either Sidearms or Longarms allows a character to avoid the penalty when using weapons within that specialty. Acquiring expertise (an enhancement) in a particular type of weapon—say, an automatic shotgun—allows the character a bonus when using that particular weapon type.

As noted in the preceding chapter, all UTRPF

Chapter 2: Skills

personnel gain Small Arms as a bonus skill.

Sidearms (Ref): Simply put, this is a specialization in combat with pistols. It includes all weapons labelled as Sidearms on the Equipment Table (page 126). Characters can take an enhancement in a particular model of Sidearm—for example, the stun pistol.

Longarms (Ref): This is a specialization in rifles, shotguns, and similar weapons. All weapons listed as Longarms on the Equipment Table (page 126) fall under this heading. Characters can take an enhancement in any particular model of Longarm.

Heavy Weapons (Ref): The Heavy Weapons skill covers the use of weapons larger and/or capable of doing more damage than are Small Arms—flame throwers, lasers, the "howler" machine gun, portable missile launchers, and indirect-fire weapons such as mortars and grenade launchers of various types. A character may choose to take an enhancement in the flame thrower, sniper laser, or howler machine gun or to specialize in one of the following.

Anti-Armor Weapons (Fit): This specialty includes not only a knowledge of how to operate portable missile launchers but also a training in recognizing the weakest spots of armored targets, so as to achieve maximum penetration.

Grenade Launchers (Fit): This specialty covers the use of firearms that fire grenades. In the BUGHUNTERS™ game, this can apply either to a grenade launcher mounted integrally under a longarm such as an assault rifle or one used as an independent weapon. In any case, all weapons that fall under this specialty are hand-carried and fired without a stabilizing mount such as a bipod.

Note that this skill can be used to fire grenades either directly at a target in line of sight or to launch them indirectly, mortar-fashion.

Mortars (Int): The Mortars specialty provides a character with the skill necessary for assembling, aiming, and firing mortars, generally indirectly at an unseen target, at the instruction of a forward observer (generally a radio operator).

Autofire (Fit): Autofire is an excellent means of suppressing enemy movement: the sheer noise is sufficient to keep most creatures hugging the ground, especially those who recognize that it means lots of flying lead. And pretty much anyone can use an autofire weapon for this purpose.

But despite its usefulness as suppressive fire, most people find it extremely difficult to hit much of anything with an autofire weapon. For that reason, all attacks with autofire are made by rolling versus the Autofire skill, rather than the usual Small Arms or Heavy Weapons skill for that weapon. Characters can take an enhancement in a particular model of weapon capable of autofire, representing their familiarity with the "kick" that particular weapon puts out when in autofire mode.

Attack rolls when using autofire are rolled versus the firer's Fitness, even when firing a weapon which usually requires a Reflexes check. Characters with the Autofire skill subtract 30 points from their Fit score; characters without the Autofire skill must first halve their Fit score and **then** subtract the 30 points.

Humanities

Under this heading, we have collected primarily skills representative of human culture, including a few not normally considered as humanities per se, such as Bureaucracy, Law, and Sports. Xenological Theory is also included here, under the premise that humans define such things in relation to themselves. Many of these will benefit PCs in role-playing, as opposed to combat, situations.

Art (Int): This skill includes both a knowledge of art history and the practical ability to create artworks (e.g., as a hobby).

Bureaucracy (Int): The Bureaucracy skill involves a familiarity with the typical trails of paperwork required to get many things done in a corporate or government office. As such, it allows a character a sense of when to push for action (when people are dragging their heels)

Chapter 2: Skills

and when to relax and let the wheels turn (or risk offending someone and causing an even longer delay). It can be very valuable when applying for a promotion or a change to a new MSO.

Cooking (Int): This skill allows a character to care for, prepare, and serve food. That may sound mundane, but as explained in the previous chapter, UTRPF cooks bear a lot of responsibility for the psychological well-being of their crews. As any soldier can tell you, meals serve as more than mere food: they are a natural focus for camaraderie, whether troopers are trading combat rations in a foxhole or sharing a banquet at a ship's table, and they serve as at least a minor break from tension or tedium. UTRPF cooks, by capitalizing upon these aspects of meals, can have a major effect upon the morale of their comrades.

Note that while characters may not have many opportunities to actually roll versus this skill, their Cooking rating should serve as an indicator of how satisfied (or dissatisfied) their crewmates are, on the whole, with the food they provide.

History (Lea): A knowledge of history can be of great help in dealing with situations. As a primary example, knowledge of the background of a particular culture or race can aid in the understanding of its members. Players can spend a skill option to specify an enhancement in a specific area of history.

Law (Lea): Under the leadership of the offices of United Terra, the Earth is more unified than at any point before in its history, and this is due in a large part to the existence of a United Terra charter establishing a unified international law. This skill denotes familiarity with that law and how it applies to specific situations on and off Terra.

However, just as each state in the United States has its own local law, specific to the needs of that locale, as do each county and city, so too do the various national and corporate members of United Terra retain the right to legislate within their own environs. Such local laws are always considered to be supplementary to, and not con-tradictory of, the body of law above them.

Characters may thus choose to take an enhancement specialty of the Law skill by focusing on a particular field or locale. A character might choose to be expert in United States national law, for instance, or Sony corporate law, or New York City civic law. The focus may be as wide or narrow as a player desires (subject to GM approval, of course).

Linguistics (Lea): Linguistics is the study of what makes languages work. As such, it can be of great use in codifying a language and tracing its historical development, but it does not automatically confer upon its possessor the ability to speak that language. It does, however, allow a person to more quickly understand the theory of a language, which has two game effects: 1) Persons who have the Linguistics skill and who fail a skill roll versus a particular language they know may immediately try the roll a second time, representing a heightened awareness of what went wrong; and 2) Linguists may puzzle out the rough meanings of languages they have never encountered before, provided they have sufficient data and time. Typically, this means at least a few days with a speaking subject or with a text containing illustrations and/or diagrams of some sort to provide a starting point.

Literature (Int): This is a knowledge of influential written works and the major theories concerning their influence.

Writing (Cha): This specialty reflects the ability to write entertainingly and effectively. Its primary application involves the creation of works of poetry, drama, and fiction.

Music (Int): The Music skill allows a character to understand and enjoy music to a greater degree than is usual and to sing more effectively. It also serves as a precursor to learning a musical instrument.

Instrument (Cha): This specialty represents skill in playing a particular musical instrument. The character who takes this specialty must identify the instrument being learned. The specialty may be taken more than once to represent

Chapter 2: Skills

skill in several different instruments.

Philosophy (Lea): This is a knowledge of essential questions of cultural value systems and their possible answers. If used in conjunction with Xenological Theory, it can be useful in gaining an understanding of alien cultures.

Protocol (Int): Unlike Bureaucracy (see above), which deals with paperwork, Protocol deals with formalities of etiquette and ceremony, with a particular emphasis upon relations between normal and synthetic humans. Given the inherent fear and hostility a great many normal humans feel toward synthetic ones, this skill can be an extremely important tool in avoiding serious conflicts.

Religion (Lea): This skill involves a familiarity with beliefs in the supernatural and the systems of worship that arise around them. Characters can choose a specialization in a specific religious faith in order to gain a skill bonus when dealing with that faith in particular.

Sports (Lea): To some extent, sports give a cul-

ture definition, allowing its citizens a chance to rally together around specific teams or individuals. Sports also provide a ready means of keeping in physical shape and of working out tension and aggression in a relatively safe medium.

This skill gives a character the necessary knowledge of a game's rules and traditions. Actual competition in a particular sport will generally involve tests of a character's Athletics skill (see Physical Disciplines, below). A character can use an enhancement bonus to focus on a particular type of sport.

Xenological Theory (Int): It is difficult, if not impossible, for humans to imagine something truly different from anything they have ever experienced before. But projections of what such a thing might be like can help prepare individuals to more readily come to grips with such otherness.

Xenological Theory, then, is a skill of recognizing familiar elements in alien beings, and of using them as a basis upon which to acclimate oneself to the remaining differences. More simply put, it is a training in predicting alien natures. It is intended to be used as an adjunct to other skills. For example, if used with Linguistics, it allows for the learning of alien languages; if used with Philosophy, it allows for the understanding of alien philosophies; and so on. In each case, the character must roll versus the lower of the two skills in question.

Languages

All BUGHUNTERS™ game PCs speak English, having had that language imprinted upon their minds just prior to their synthetic "birth." The following list is supplied for players who wish to round out their characters by giving them one or more additional languages.

The following are the most common languages in the early 22nd century: Arabic, neo-Bantu, Bengali, Cantonese, English, French, German, Hindustani, Italian, Japanese, Korean, Malay-Indonesian, Mandarin, Marathi, Portuguese, Punjabi, Russian, Spanish, Tamil, Tel-

Chapter 2: Skills

ugu, Turkish, Vietnamese, and Wu. Characters may, of course, pick other languages if they wish. Each language is counted as a separate skill.

Medicine

Medical knowledge has advanced greatly by the early 22nd century—as evidenced by the fact that it is possible to create cloned humans. An effective treatment has been devised for pretty much every disease common to humanity—whether bacterial, viral, or genetic in origin—through the application of nanotechnology, and great expertise has been developed in the repair of accidental damage. As a result, most citizens of Earth have a very good chance of living to be 110 to 120 years of age, barring accident far from medical facilities.

That's where the problem arises. Off-Earth, medical facilities may be much less accessible and the risks of injury much higher. In particular, combat troops such as UTRPF soldiers are prone to an early death. The central lesson taught to every UTRPF trainee is: "Stay sharp; stay cool; stay in contact with base; and stay in the doc's good graces" (the last, of course, is merely humor). The biggest deciding factors affecting survival in cases of injury are how close the patient is to a well-stocked medical facility and how good the field medic is.

The following are those skills a field medic or ship's doctor will typically use.

First Aid (Int): The First Aid skill is concerned with two basic areas of need. The first concerns treatment of minor problems such as scratches, insect bites, rashes, sunburn, athlete's foot, blisters, and the like. The second focuses on treatment of life-threatening emergencies so as to avoid shock and stabilize a patient for transportation back to a medical facility, where more extensive treatment and repair of damage can be performed.

Chapter 4: Combat and Repair details exactly how these effects of First Aid are translated into game terms.

General Medicine (Lea): General Medicine is a very broad-ranging skill, covering everything from treatment of viral infections to the delivery of babies. Often, a general practitioner will make an initial diagnosis of a condition, then refer the patient to a specialist in that field. Much of a general practitioner's job involves prescribing medications.

In BUGHUNTERS™ game terms, General Medicine is the most critical skill for ships' doctors. Possession of one or more of the specialties listed below can be of great aid, of course, but a well-stocked sick bay includes computer programs to assist a general practitioner in these areas.

Emergency Medicine (Lea): This specialty is of particular usefulness in treating acute, life-threatening situations. Its specific game effects are covered in Chapter 4: Combat and Repair.

Psychiatry (Lea): The isolation of space, and the horrific nature of many of the inhabitants of other worlds, can have an extremely deleterious effect on the human psyche. This specialty allows for the treatment of such troubles. *Characters desiring this skill must first possess the Psychology specialty from the Sciences pool.*

Stasis Medicine (Lea): Most of the time, characters revive from stasis sleep quite easily, once a stasis pod's automatic revival sequence has been initiated. But on occasion, someone will slip into a stasis coma, and it requires a great deal of medical skill and understanding of stasis sleep to revive such an individual. The Stasis Medicine specialty represents that skill.

Surgery (Lea): Surgical knowledge and skill has expanded greatly by the time of the early 22nd century. Surgical lasers, advanced optics, computer assistance, nanotechnology, cloned organs, and biological sealers have made even limb replacement and nerve repair possible. The trauma of surgery is much less than it was a century and a half before, promoting faster recovery times for patients.

Synthetic Medicine (Lea): As synthetic humans, synners sometimes require medical

Chapter 2: Skills

treatment somewhat different from that of normal humans. This specialty reflects a specialization in those differences. In game terms, it operates somewhat differently from other specialties, giving a bonus of +20 to any and all medical skill use concerning a synthetic human patient. In effect, it serves as an enhancement to all other medical skills.

Military

Collected within this skill pool are skills with primarily military applications.

Comm Gear (Int): The Comm Gear skill covers a basic familiarity with radio and video communications equipment, especially that typically used in field operations.

Comm Procedure (Lea): Military and paramilitary units have particular communications protocols to make certain that messages are conveyed quickly and accurately while at the same time ensuring minimal information to any enemy that might be eavesdropping. This involves standard pronunciation, abbreviations, codes, call-in times, transmission lengths, and the like.

The Comm Procedure specialty covers exactly that sort of knowledge. It also allows a radio operator to act as a forward observer for indirect fire (e.g., mortar) by transmitting coordinates, observing the resulting fire, and radioing corrections.

Isler Radio (Lea): The Isler Radio specialization allows a character to operate an Isler Radio, a device that instantaneously conveys radio-like transmissions through hyperspace over very long distances at a very great energy expenditure. Because of the high technology required to build and operate them, and because of their high energy demands, Isler Radios can only be found at those few facilities where the expense can be met and the energy provided. Currently, there is one on Earth at UT headquarters in New York City, a second in UTRPF HQ on Stargate, and a third at New Austin on Acey-Two.

Demolitions (Lea): The Demolitions skill allows a character to accurately judge the amount of explosive needed for a particular task —whether that be opening a hole in a rock face, sealing a cave entrance, destroying a building, or what have you. It enables the person with the skill to place the explosive accurately and to set it off without being blown to kingdom come.

Environmental Suit (Int): This skill conveys the ability to don and operate in enclosed protective gear, whether it be spacesuits, deep-sea diving gear, or other hostile environment gear.

Gunnery (Int): Gunnery is the skill of operating a spacecraft's laser guns and nuclear missiles. In some cases, it involves targets as simple as a fixed-orbit satellite. At its most difficult, it may involve combat between ships cycling rapidly into and out of hyperspace, at incredible speeds and distances. Obviously, a great deal of computer assistance is required to hit anything in such situations, and the Gunnery skill includes the knowledge of how to operate those programs to best effect.

The Gunnery skill is also needed in order to correctly set up the motion-sensing repeating auto-laser (the "Disco Light") often used for perimeter defense.

Leadership (Cha): This is the skill of motivating a group of people to follow a particular plan, often in the face of adversity. It is of extreme importance for military officers.

Military Science (Lea): The Military Science skill reflects a knowledge of military history, with a particular emphasis on strategy and tactics. It allows its possessor a chance to predict what an enemy will do in a given situation and to recognize what reactions would be most effective. In game terms, this will usually mean that the GM gives the character further insight into the opposing forces. Alternatively, a GM may decide to simply give the character a bonus to rolls for advantage and/or initiative.

Chapter 2: Skills

Personality

The following skills are dependent primarily upon the Charm attribute, reflecting their dependence upon a winning personality.

Bluffing (Cha): This is the skill of convincing someone to act on mistaken beliefs. Usually, the bluffer either professes to a falsehood in such a way that the hearer believes it to be true, or the bluffer professes to a truth in such a way that the hearer believes it to be false. Sometimes bluffers can accomplish this without speaking a word, merely by letting their victims talk themselves into believing something that is not so.

Bargaining (Cha): Bargaining is the skill of making deals in such a manner that both buyer and seller believe they got the better of the other. In game terms, this specialty means persuading someone to sell you something for less than they are asking or to buy something from you for more than they first offer.

Gambling (Cha): Although the Gambling specialty depends upon the Bluffing skill, it involves as well a knowledge of odds and a sense of how to exploit them.

Luck (Psy): In BUGHUNTERS™ adventures, this skill serves primarily as a last-ditch chance to save a character's life in a deadly situation. Whenever a character takes sufficient damage to die or fails a roll necessary for survival (such as to avoid puncturing a space suit or to leap across a "bottomless" chasm) the character's player may attempt a Luck roll.

In cases involving damage sufficient to kill the character, a successful Luck roll means the character is reduced to a single body point. If any stamina points remain to the character, the individual remains conscious, as well.

In cases involving "do or die" rolls—such as the chasm mentioned above—a successful Luck roll means that the character had some truly amazing stroke of fortune, something dramatically appropriate to the situation. A character who failed to jump the chasm might fortuitously land on a precarious ledge part-way down, for instance. The badly-injured character will still

have to figure out a way of escaping from the ledge and regaining the surface, but this is a minor price to pay for having eluded certain death. In the case of the character with the punctured airsuit, some small object in the character's pocket—say a notepad computer—might get stuck in the hole, blocking the rush of air long enough for the lucky individual to get to an airlock and into a new suit. In each such case the character takes damage (in the examples, from falling and decompression, respectively) but nevertheless manages to just barely survive. GMs should use their imaginations in all such situations and are encouraged to ask the players to suggest ideas.

Street Smarts (Cha): This is the skill of communicating effectively with denizens of urban streets, of recognizing certain settings as safe or unsafe, and of knowing how and where to seek things. It could be called the skill of urban survival. It can be extremely useful to characters contemplating any missions to Earth.

Chapter 2: Skills

Trivia (Wil): Trivia is the skill of recalling seemingly insignificant facts at the appropriate moment. It is usually of value only as entertainment, but it can serve as a mechanic for the GM to justify a character having noticed something important and recalling it at a critical point in time. Trivia can be used in conjunction with any other skill a character possesses to tell a yarn related to that other skill.

Physical Disciplines

The following skills are primarily physical in nature, as evidenced by their relation to the Physique attributes.

Armed Combat (Ref): This is the skill of fighting in melee combat with hand-held weapons such as bayonets, clubs, knives, or even bricks, rocks, and broken bottles.

Characters may specialize in combat with a particular type of hand weapon in order to improve their skill when fighting with that particular weapon type.

Athletics (Ref): This is a skill of knowing generally how to move quickly, dodge opponents, roll with falls, maintain balance, etc. In game terms, it allows a character to roll twice for most tests of the Reflexes attribute (subject to GM determination but never including attacks by the character making the roll) and take the better of the two rolls.

Brawling (Fit): As an unarmed melee combat skill, Brawling depends primarily upon brute force rather than elegance of movement to achieve its effect.

Climbing (Ref): This skill represents expertise in climbing vertical surfaces of all types, including familiarity with climbing gear and recognition of good handholds and footholds. The GM will determine how many Climbing checks must be made to scale a surface; the more difficult the surface, the more frequent the rolls. As a general rule, in normal gravity, one check should be made every 20 meters. The GM may assign penalties for lack of appropriate gear.

Grappling (Ref): This is the skill of grappling an opponent's limb (such as a gun hand) in combat or even of pinning the opponent completely.

High-G Maneuver (Fit): Gravities from 1.2 G to 2.0 G pose special hazards for characters who attempt to stand or move about within them (gravities over 2.0 G are considered too heavy for characters to do much of anything in them). For one thing, the human cardio-vascular system is not designed to pump blood effectively in such gravities, and people have a tendency to black out from diminished blood supply to the brain unless they remain prone and motionless. For another, there is an increased chance of musculo-skeletal injury from an awkward step or a fall. Characters with the High-G Maneuver skill have been specially trained to deal with high-G environments.

In game terms, whenever characters fail at any sort of Fitness or Reflexes skill check in a high-G environment, they must make an immediate High-G Maneuver check. A character who fails this check suffers a loss of 2d6 stamina points. If this causes the character to become unconscious, an additional 1d6 body point loss is accrued from the subsequent fall.

Low-G Maneuver (Ref): Low-G environments pose their own special set of problems for characters. Primarily, these are problems involving maintaining balance, given the awkward combination of diminished weight with the same mass, lessening of traction, and the bulky environmental suits often required; recoil from weapon fire also poses a considerable problem. As a result, the Low-G Maneuver skill serves as a limiter for physical skill attempts. That is, whenever characters attempt a Fitness or Reflexes skill roll in a low-G environment, they must roll instead versus the Low-G Maneuver skill, if that value is lower. Characters without the Low-G Maneuver skill cannot have scores higher than half their Reflexes in such situations.

Swimming (Fit): This skill allows a character to swim. Top speed is one-fourth of the Fitness score (rounded down) in meters per combat round. This speed can only be maintained for a

Chapter 2: Skills

number of rounds equal to one-tenth the character's Willpower (also rounded down). Characters can swim longer distances, at a progressively slower pace, up to a number of kilometers equal to their Fitness, although a Willpower check must be made for every 10 km swum in order to continue.

Throwing (Ref): The Throwing skill allows characters to hurl items; it is typically used in combat to throw grenades, knives, rocks, etc. Further explanation of the skill's use is given in the Combat chapter.

A character may take an enhancement for a particular type of object (throwing knives, for instance) and gain a bonus to Throwing skill attempts.

Unarmed Combat (Ref): Whereas Brawling depends primarily upon brute strength, other types of unarmed fighting depend upon speed, accuracy of strikes and blocks, and knowledge of important target areas on an opponent's body. In the BUGHUNTERS™ game, they are represented by the Unarmed Combat skill. Specifics of damage done in unarmed fighting are given in Chapter 4: Combat and Repair.

A character may devote a skill choice to a particular style of martial art (judo, ju jitsu, or whatever) and gain an enhancement bonus when fighting with Unarmed Combat.

Sciences

Most citizens of a technological society know more about science than they might at first suspect. For that reason, in the BUGHUNTERS game the General Sciences skill has been related to the Intuition attribute, to allow for some chance of its use even by characters who do not specifically have the skill.

The specialties listed below that skill are frequently called the "hard" sciences, because their precepts can be readily demonstrated by experimentation (as opposed to "soft" sciences such as anthropology and sociology). Note that psychology, which during the 20th century was considered a "soft" science, has by the 22nd century received greater acceptance as a "hard" science, due to improved understanding of brain chemistry and function (though there are yet some who would deny its place within that group).

General Sciences (Int): This skill reflects a level of scientific knowledge equivalent to that of most college graduates. Of course, the Intuition attribute of individuals possessing this skill demonstrates the variance within that group.

Biology (Lea): A knowledge of biological function in all its myriad forms is the focus of this specialty.

Chemistry (Lea): This specialty gives an expert level of understanding of chemical theory, from basic molecular to organic.

Physics (Lea): This specialty provides a deep familiarity with the natural laws of the universe and of advances in hyperspace theory.

Psychology (Lea): The understanding of the human mind and emotions are covered by this specialty.

Travel

As evidenced by the names of the two primary skills listed below, this skill pool involves piloting vehicles and navigating one's way through various different environments.

Navigation, Planetary (Int): This skill reflects a knowledge of how to use maps and landmarks so as to navigate from one location to another across the surface of a planet, asteroid, or moon. It takes into account such things as the position of the planet's magnetic pole to determine cardinal directions, typically depending not so much upon a knowledge of objects in the skies as upon those on the ground.

Space Navigation (Lea): This specialization concerns navigation primarily through interplanetary space. It requires a thorough knowledge of stellar positions and of the relative positions of solar bodies. The skill is extremely important in plotting courses within a solar system, taking into account both the acceleration and direction needed in order to match a vessel's vector with that of its target. These calculations are of course

Chapter 2: Skills

further complicated by the fact that the target will always be in motion due to the effects of gravitation, so that its vector will continually be changing.

Fortunately, space navigators have at their disposal excellent sighting instruments and computer programs to aid in their work.

Hyperspace Navigation (Lea): If navigating through interplanetary space is difficult, doing so through the interstellar reaches during hyperspace travel is definitely more so and depends upon specialization in Hyperspace Navigation. The perceived positions and brightnesses of stars are constantly changing as a vessel travels, eventually forming new constellations unfamiliar to human experience. And the sheer amount of emptiness between the stars makes interplanetary distances seem paltry by comparison. The computer assistance needed for such navigation becomes ever more critical the further a vessel travels from Earth.

Piloting, Surface (Int): Over the centuries, controls for planetary vehicles have become ever more user-friendly, and drivers ever more educated in their use. As a result, pretty much anyone in the 22nd century can pilot a wheeled ground vehicle, and nautical vessels and hovercraft are barely more difficult. Typically, no skill test is needed for piloting such craft.

The Surface Piloting skill reflects a better than average expertise in driving planetary vehicles, especially during critical situations when skill checks become necessary, such as high-speed chases.

A character may choose to take an enhancement in a particular type of planetary vehicle, such as hovercraft, motorcycles, or speed boats.

Aerospace Piloting (Lea): Piloting across the ground or water is one thing; piloting through air or the vacuum of interplanetary space is quite another. This specialty allows a character to pilot such flying vehicles.

A character may choose to specialize in a particular aerospace vehicle type—such as helicopter, fixed-wing, orbital, or interplanetary—in order to gain an enhancement bonus to skill tests with that type.

Hyperspace Piloting (Lea): Piloting an Isler Drive vessel through hyperspace jumps is a difficult business, requiring an expertise above and beyond other types of piloting.

Other Skills

The skills list above has been designed to match the needs of—and convey the atmosphere of—the BUGHUNTERS™ game milieu. Naturally, many possible skills have been left out of this list as of too-limited a use to be justified.

However, role-playing gamers are always full of surprises, and individual campaigns tend to take on a distinctive character of their own. Consequently, some players may find themselves desiring skills for their PCs that are not listed here. GMs are free to add any new skills they believe necessary, and players are encouraged to make suggestions along those lines.

The final decisions of whether or not a new skill should be included, and exactly how and when it will work, rest on individual GMs, for their own campaigns.

Chapter 3:
Playing the Role

If you are going to play the part of an UTRPF trooper, you'll need to know how synners think. This chapter discusses many of the unique conditions surrounding synners, thereby providing insights into their mindset.

The Dwellers in Limbo

The single most significant fact about synner psychology is that they each and every one feel dispossessed, cut off from all they have previously known. It is a situation worse than having no roots at all—synners have memories of homes, friends, lovers, parents, and even children but are painfully aware that they can never return into that fold. As much as they might long to reclaim that history, they know that someone else—their donor—holds that place, and that knowledge is a constant reminder that they are, themselves, merely copies of the person they feel themselves to be.

What's more, the self-image synners have carried over from their earlier life no longer matches with what they see in the mirror each day. Were they old? Now they are young. Were they scrawny or obese? Now they are trim and muscular. Did they bear scars? Now they have the perfect, smooth skin of the newly born.

To synners, these things are constant reminders that they are something other than fully human. From the time they are decanted, they know that they have been created to fulfill a need for the human race. Having human memories, they know all too well that humans have cause to fear their more-than-human strength and durability. And although UTRPF might play word games to avoid directly saying so, synners know that they are considered to be a specialized type of equipment rather than thinking, feeling individuals.

Worst of all, they know that it was, in effect, their own decision that brought them to this pass, for they can never forget signing up to donate tissue and memories to UTRPF in their "past life."

Against these self-recriminations and feelings of dispossession, synners have only two weapons. The first is the duty and discipline taught to them by UTRPF. Like soldiers everywhere, they avoid loneliness by subordinating themselves to their role as soldiers. The second weapon is the camaraderie of other synners. As has been said many times, "Misery loves company." Living and working with other clones establishes an essential interpersonal support. For this reason, synners tend to be fiercely loyal to others of their kind, almost clannish—a fact that has led many human officers who command them to characterize synths as cold and unfriendly, furthering bias against clones and rumors of their essential inhumanity.

This is not to say that drawing together is always easy. Because of the widely divergent backgrounds from which many UTRPF donors come, often with extreme differences in age and experience, individual synners may face terrible difficulties in relating to others of their kind. But given that they have no real choice but to adapt, virtually all learn to do so. Synners can actually claim as one of the true benefits of their situation the broad-mindedness that comes as a result of seriously considering very different viewpoints.

Conversely, overly similar backgrounds can cause as much initial trouble as overly dissimilar ones. Sometimes friends and lovers will come as donors to UTRPF together. Faced with the alienation of synner existence, their clones may initially cling too closely to one another before looking outward to develop a healthy dependence upon synner society as a whole.

And while most synners eventually come to rely upon duty and camaraderie as twin pillars of support, becoming psychologically well-adjusted to their situation, only a very very few of them ever really shake entirely the nagging pain of the fact that they are copies of someone else, and that the Earth doesn't want them as citizens. On occasion, this pushes an individual over the brink of madness.

Chapter 3: Playing the Role

Daily Life

Exactly what a synner's day is like depends entirely upon where that individual is currently assigned.

At the main UTRPF compound on Stargate, a synner's life is pretty much taken up by daily drill and training, with evenings and weekends free for personal pursuits within the compound. Those pastimes are as varied as the clone's donor backgrounds, ranging from writer's groups and literary circles to theater-going, bowling, or raucous partying. Because it contains UTRPF HQ, Stargate is also the best place for a synner to learn new MSOs and test for promotion.

Generally, synners are only allowed on Earth in one of three cases. The first is if there is some need for their services, such as heavy backup for police teams facing a particularly difficult situation. The second is in UTRPF tour groups, which are run upon occasion to remind synners of the (sometimes dubious) beauties of the home world they protect. In both of these situations, very close tabs are kept on the UTRPF troopers, and they are kept from any serious interaction with the local population as much as possible, in order to avoid potential conflicts. The third case is the extremely rare occasion in which a synner goes rogue and somehow manages to return to Earth to hide among the planet's masses, in which event a team of clone troopers is sent to hunt down the renegade. Civilian populations tend to be very tense in such situations, making this one of the most dangerous missions a synner can be assigned to, with the possibility of violence both from the fugitive and the frightened local populace.

On colony and outpost worlds, human attitudes toward synners are often more relaxed and less antagonistic. Many colonists were themselves something of misfits back on Earth; others are among humanity's brightest and least prejudiced. And in any event, life on these worlds is tough enough that any pair of hands is welcome to join the work, clone or not. What's more, as these remote spots of habitation are beginning to fall under attack from hostile outside forces, a visit by combat-experienced UTRPF troopers is becoming an increasingly more welcome event.

Acey-Two—Humanity's one full-fledged colony world beyond the Solar System—is something of a special case in this regard. The planet is extremely Earth-like, though quite wild, with room enough at present for pretty much anyone to set up a homestead. On occasion, UTRPF troops are sent to construct new bases on this planet, preparatory to the influx of a batch of new colonists. A few older synners with excellent service records have even been allowed to retire to reserve status; they remain on UTRPF's duty rosters as "consultants" and are subject to recall at any time if the need arises. Such synners may even have homesteads of their own and be accepted as unofficial citizens of one village or another.

Of course, a great deal of an UTRPF trooper's time is spent in interstellar travel. These are considered times of real glory by most synners. The voyages take months, or even years, to accomplish, and during this time synners are completely free from the presence of normal humans (unless carrying a "meatwagon" full of people in stasis, who hardly count as a presence). They are dependent only upon one another, at liberty to enjoy the beauty of hyperspace travel and ruminate upon the unbelievable immensity of the universe. It can be a lonely time, but a wonderfully soul-healing one—as stargazers since the dawn of time would certainly predict—and most synners welcome it readily.

Missions

UTRPF HQ has two approaches to the assembly of mission teams. The primary one is what would be expected of any military force: they assign individuals to fill specific slots in standard squads, platoons, companies, etc., then order an appropriately sized and equipped group to whatever mission comes up. This is UTRPF's

Chapter 3: Playing the Role

standard approach to fielding moderate-to-large forces. But for situations that require smaller groups, such as the relatively cramped quarters of long-distance star travel, higher command is becoming increasingly prone to building mission teams around groups of synners who already spend their free time together as friends, then allotting extra personnel only as strictly necessary to fill critical slots such as Pilot. It is into this latter team approach that PCs tend to fall, although they may well find themselves pressed into service as part of a larger force from time to time.

Mission Training: Training for missions involves several different things. First, there is the daily training and practice that soldiers undergo in order to remain efficient at general military tasks. This includes everything from physical workouts and marksmanship drills to classwork and written tests. Second, when enough advance notice is possible, troopers are drilled in unusual skills appropriate to a particular mission, such as parachuting or space-walking.

One of the more interesting training possibilities, however, involves the use of virtual reality technology, facilitated by the mental recording equipment whereby clones are given their initial memories. Upon occasion, for missions regarded as unusually difficult or critical, UTRPF HQ will prepare a virtual reality simulation of the projected mission, then put the mission team through it as a special dry run. By monitoring and manipulating brain activity via the mental recording equipment, they can make this dry run seem extremely real to the characters undergoing the training. This gives troopers a chance to become accustomed to an unfamiliar environment and learn from their mistakes before tackling the actual mission.

In game terms, a virtual reality mission is run like any other. At the beginning of the adventure your GM may or may not tell you that it is virtual reality rather than an actual mission. To represent the benefit of such a dry run, experience points may be gained on the virtual reality

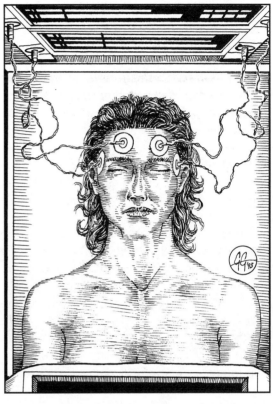

adventure, but they are subject to the following three restrictions:

1) they can only be spent during the subsequent real mission,

2) they can only be used to gain die roll modifiers for skill checks, not to gain some permanent benefit, and

3) they can only be used if the actual mission bears some resemblance to the simulation.

Of course, the greatest benefit of such a training mission is that mistakes can be made without people actually dying.

Note that synners can always request a virtual reality dry run prior to an actual mission, but the request may be denied because of lack of programming time before the actual mission or because a mission is deemed unworthy of the trouble. In other words, your GM will decide whether or not to approve the request.

Chapter 4:
Combat & Repair

Engineer Kruk snapped off a piece of the corroded hull and crumbled it between her fingers. "It's some corrosive element secreted by the plant's roots," she said.

We'd landed in this jungle hell-hole just twelve hours earlier, but in the time it had taken to scout out the ruins of what had been a human outpost and fight off one attack by a nightmarish, burrowing monstrosity this fine, ivy-like plant had engulfed the ship, leaving behind a useless, fuzzy wreck. "We'll never get back into orbit in this thing. And that stuff'll grow over us, too, if we don't keep moving," added Kruk.

"This ain't my MSO, Kruk, but considering that there are xenos around here, I'd better take charge," Corporal Yuan said, readying his assault rifle. She nodded. With the captain carried off by the burrower and the ship now destroyed, the aerospace folks felt safer with the marines calling the shots.

"Fan out. Get me a perimeter," Yuan ordered, and the grunts obeyed. "Scout us a track to the high ground, and make it snappy, before the local greenery makes lunch out of us, too."

Before the last grunt was even out of sight, several bursts of autofire tore through the foliage in front of us. Incoherent screaming issued through our headsets. Yuan cursed and tossed me a weapon.

"What's this?" I asked, turning the thing end over end.

"A grenade launcher. Get ready to use it!"

My immediate, panicked thought was <u>there's never a manual around when you need one</u>.

In the BUGHUNTERS™ game, combat can take many forms in many different situations. A well-organized outfit of marines can penetrate a strange alien vessel and battle the xenos within. Or those same marines can get caught in ambush on the face of a distant planet. From spaceship corridors to open ice plains, with high tech weaponry or armed with little more than a pointed stick, a UTRPF soldier's life is never dull. The AMAZING ENGINE™ game *System Guide* covers all the basics of combat. What follows are the particular exceptions and expansions to those rules made necessary by the BUGHUNTERS game environment.

The Combat Sequence

Regardless of the environment, shipboard or planetside, surprise is an important element in BUGHUNTERS game combat. Ambushes are common on both sides: UTRPF soldiers setting a trap to capture a single alien for analysis by the folks back at Edison Point, or a dozen xenos camouflaged in the mossy warrens of their homeworld, waiting for the right moment to strike at the intruding synners. Often surprise is the deciding factor in determining who lives and dies in an encounter, requiring the following additions to the advantage and initiative rules of the *System Guide*.

Advantage

In BUGHUNTERS adventures, advantage is determined basically as described in the *System Guide*: both sides check against the highest Psyche score in their party; those passing the check are forewarned of the coming encounter.

Ambushes require slightly specialized treatment, however. In an ambush situation, the ambushers gain a +10 modifier to Psyche for purposes of this check and are surprised only on a failed roll with a failure margin of F9. Characters being ambushed suffer a –10 modifier to Psyche for purposes of the advantage roll and are surprised on a failed roll with a failure margin of F8.

Note that the GM can adjust the Psyche modifiers to reflect the fact that creatures and soldiers alike have a worse chance of conducting or detecting an ambush when in an unfamiliar environment. For example, aliens waiting in their own environment are not likely to be surprised by approaching UTRPF troopers. However, a handful of xenos that have escaped their

Chapter 4:
Combat & Repair

cages in an L-5 laboratory are out of their normal environment and, therefore, much more vulnerable to surprise.

The effects of advantage and surprise are as explained on pages 25-26 of the AMAZING ENGINE™ game *System Guide.*

Declaring Actions

BUGHUNTERS™ game combat actions can be more detailed or more complicated than in other AMAZING ENGINE games, but the process is essentially the same. Each character declares to the GM a course of action for the turn **before knowing in what order both sides will act.** Combat rounds are 10 seconds in length; actions should be limited to things that could be accomplished in that amount of time. As a guide, characters can combine one action option with one movement option into a single course of action for the turn. In addition, there are a few special maneuvers that may be allowed in combination with other things.

The box below explains which action options can be combined with which movement options. Movement rates, summarized on page 128 of this book, are explained in more detail in the *System Guide* (pages 22-23); action options (divided into Hand-to-Hand Actions and Ranged Actions) and special maneuvers are explained in the appropriate portions of this chapter. Note that some movement rates may incur penalties to ranged attacks (see page 49).

Initiative

Combat situations in the BUGHUNTERS game can be extremely complicated, and the order in which each character acts is extremely important. Unlike in most AMAZING ENGINE games, a separate initiative number is generated for each and every character in combat.

To determine the order in which character actions occur, the GM and each player roll a single 10-sided die. Players each add to their die roll their character's initiative modifier (the tens digit of the character's Reflexes score), thereby generating a personal initiative rating. The GM's creatures each apply their individual initiative modifier to the GM's single roll—rolling only one die keeps things simpler for the GM, while still generating individual initiative numbers for the creatures.

The character or NPC with the highest rating goes first, the one with the next highest score

---

Action Options by Movement Type

Stationary: Any action.
Walk: Any action except aimed fire.
Run: Any hand-to-hand action; no ranged action except throw weapon, burst fire, or autofire.
Sprint: No action but tackle.

Chapter 4:
Combat & Repair

second, and so forth. Consequently, it is common in combat for the order of actions to bounce back and forth from one side to the other.

Some combat suits impose initiative modifiers, as do many hand-to-hand weapons; these are covered in the individual descriptions in the next chapter. Also, both high- and low-gravity situations may adversely affect a character's Reflexes and Fitness checks, unless the individual has equipment or skills to negate their effects.

Hitting Your Target

The basics of hitting a target are explained in the AMAZING ENGINE™ game *System Guide*. Rules specific to BUGHUNTERS™ game combat are as follows.

Target Areas

Characters without xenobiology skill, or first hand experience, can only guess as to the vital or non-vital areas of an alien creature. A xenobiologist has the necessary knowledge to select target areas on any alien, given a chance to observe the creature and make the necessary deductions. Also, troopers who have already encountered a particular alien species may learn from experience and target vital or non-vital spots as they wish (the GM is, of course, the final arbiter in deciding whether or not this knowledge applies in any given situation). All other characters must use the following "New Bug" Targeting rules.

"New Bug" Targeting: General targeting is unrestricted against a newly discovered alien creature. However, characters who want to target either vital or non-vital locations must trust to their Intuition, rolling against that score. If successful, the targeting is correct. Otherwise, the targeting is exactly the opposite of what was desired—i.e., a vital shot hits a non-vital area or vice versa. GMs may modify an attacker's Intuition score by +10% if a target creature is bipedal or roughly humanoid in shape.

Hand-to-Hand Actions

The following actions are typical of hand-to-hand combat in BUGHUNTERS adventures.

Tackle: A character may attempt to tackle an opponent. Both characters must make a test of their Reflexes attribute. If both characters succeed, the tackle hits and both fall prone, but no damage is done and no hold is established. If the tackler succeeds but the target fails, the target is knocked down with the tackler on top: both characters fall, and the target takes damage from the fall and is pinned (see "Grapple," immediately below). If the tackler fails but the target succeeds, the tackle misses; the tackler takes damage and lands prone next to the target, who remains standing. If both characters fail, the two collide; both fall and take damage, but no hold is established. Damage suffered from any of the above falls equals 1d10(1) points.

Grapple: Grappling requires a character to roll versus the Grappling skill (from the Physical Disciplines pool).

Grappling a limb requires one action to accomplish and, if successful, prevents the opponent from using the limb in question (can't aim the gun, run away, or whatever). It does not preclude the opponent from attacking with other limbs, but does quarter the chance of all other physical skill rolls by both grappler and victim succeeding, except further grappling attempts.

An opponent who has been successfully grappled can be pinned if the grappler makes a successful skill check the next round. If this check succeeds, the victim is pinned and can take no physical action other than attempt to escape. If the check fails it can be attempted again on each subsequent round, so long as the victim remains grappled.

Escaping a pin requires a test of the victim's Fitness versus the grappler's Fitness. If the victim bests the grappler at this test, the pin reverts to a grapple. Escaping a grapple requires a similar test of Fitness versus Fitness.

Strike: Striking a target in hand-to-hand com-

Chapter 4:
Combat & Repair

bat involves use of the Armed Combat, Unarmed Combat, or Brawling skills from the Physical Disciplines pool. Damage done by these attacks depends upon the weapon type (fist, foot, knife, club, etc.). These damages are summarized in the table on page 127.

Note, however, that targets of such attacks do not blithely stand still waiting to be hit. Rather, they dodge and block as best they may. To represent this, for a strike to be successful, the attacker's die roll must both be less than or equal to the attacker's appropriate skill rating *and* greater than ¼ the target's Reflexes rating. In other words, an attack roll less than or equal to ¼ the target's Reflexes rating would normally have hit, but the target dodged or blocked it.

Ranged Actions

Ranged combat in the BUGHUNTERS™ game is broken down into the following types of actions.

Throwing: To hit a target with a thrown object requires a test of the Throwing skill. To hit a target in normal gravity, characters can throw an object weighing one kilogram or less that has been designed for throwing (footballs, throwing knives, etc.) a maximum distance in meters equal to ½ their Fitness score. This is the furthest extent of long range attacks; medium range ones reach to half that distance, short range to half that.

For heavier objects, use the same system but divide the maximum attack range (½ the attacker's Fitness score) by the object's weight. Unbalanced objects can be thrown half as far as ones designed for missile use. All attack ranges are cut in half by high-G environments and doubled in low-G environments. *All modifiers are cumulative.*

A character can move as fast as a run and still make a thrown attack.

Aimed Fire: In the BUGHUNTERS game, most firearms can certainly fire more than once in a 10-second round, but by concentrating on a single shot, a character may enhance the chances of hitting a target. The aimed fire option reflects this, allowing the character only one shot for the turn, but at a bonus of +15. This makes aimed fire a desirable option when shooting at a specific target. Note that in this case, the bonus is added **before** any other modifiers to the attack percentage.

Only Small Arms weapons may be aimed, and aimed fire can only be performed by stationary characters.

Snapfire: Snapfire is the action of taking multiple, quickly aimed shots during a turn. It is the usual method of firing in combat, the default when aimed, burst, or autofire are not specified by an attacker. When performing snapfire, a character may shoot at a weapon's normal rate of fire (not its autofire rate), at the character's applicable Firearms skill. There is no special modification for this action, and shots may be fired at different targets, if desired.

Snapfire may only be performed at a speed of walk or slower. Each shot may be made from a different spot along the firing character's course of travel.

Burst Fire: Burst fire is similar to snapfire, but instead of firing single shots, a character squeezes off short bursts, at a –10 penalty to the applicable Firearms skill if walking, –30 if running. Each burst may be fired at a different target. The benefit is that burst fire doubles the weapon's damage rating and increases its lethality rating by 1. The detriment—besides the skill penalty—is that ammo is used up a bit faster.

Burst fire may only be performed at a speed no faster than a run. Each burst may be fired from a different spot along the firing character's course of travel.

Autofire: A character may use the Autofire skill to fire a weapon at up to its full automatic rate (if any). The benefits of autofire are the frightful noise produced and the chance of hitting with multiple rounds: the autofire mode quadruples the weapon's damage rating and increases its lethality rating by 3. The detriments

Chapter 4:
Combat & Repair

are increased difficulty in aiming and the extremely rapid depletion of ammunition. When autofire is conducted, a weapon uses up the amount of ammo listed as its autofire rate.

To conduct autofire, the player must remain stationary for the turn and designate *at the beginning of the turn* the area to be covered by the fire. All targets within that area are liable to attack, to a maximum number equal to one-half the number of projectiles fired. In addition, anyone entering that area for the rest of the turn, whether friend or foe, is subject to an immediate attack (this is in addition to the normal maximum number of targets). Autofire takes an entire turn, so a character cannot fire and then dive for cover, for example.

To determine the skill modifier for autofire attacks, the GM estimates the area to be covered as an arc centered upon the firer, in multiples of 45°. Arcs of 0°-45° are treated as 45°, 46°-90° are treated as 90°, and so forth, for purposes of the modifier, with a single target receiving the 45°

modifier. For each 45° of arc to be covered, the firer's attack score suffers a penalty of –30.

When determining who is hit by autofire, begin with the target closest to the attacker, proceed to the next closest, and so on. Skill penalties for targets beyond short range do apply.

Indirect Fire: Some weapons, such as grenade launchers and mortars, are designed to loft rounds over obstacles in order to hit a target or area that cannot be seen by the firer. Typically, this is done at the direction of a forward observer (FO), who radios trajectory corrections back to the firer. In such cases, both firer and FO must pass a skill test—the firer versus the Mortars specialization and the FO versus Comm Procedure—to determine whether or not the round hits the designated target. If the target is within the firer's line of sight, no FO is needed; the skill test is made only against the firer's Mortars specialization rating.

Indirect fire may not gain the Aimed Fire bonus described on page 49. Instead, it receives a targeting bonus for repeated fire. Repeated indirect fire at the same target yields a bonus of +5 to skill attempts per additional shot, to a maximum chance of 90%.

Missed shots still land somewhere. Roll 1d6 to determine direction of deviation from the target: 1 and 2 mean beyond the target; 3 means to the right; 4 and 5 mean short; and 6 means to the left. Then, to determine distance of deviation, roll 1d6 and multiply by 1/10th the range from firer to target. The round will land this distance from the target, in the direction rolled.

Indirect fire with hand-held weapons such as grenade launchers may not be conducted at any faster movement rate than a walk. Grounded weapons such as mortars may not be moved and fired in the same turn.

Reload: Reloading a weapon is an action option that may only be performed by walking or stationary characters. It typically takes a single turn to reload Small Arms, twice that for Heavy Weapons.

Chapter 4: Combat & Repair

Special Maneuvers

The following serve as examples of special maneuvers that may be included in a course of action. Several such maneuvers may be combined, subject to GM approval and depending upon the circumstances.

Stand: This includes rising from a prone or kneeling position.

Kneel: Kneeling may allow a character to take advantage of short cover, and it provides a slightly more stable platform for fire (+5 bonus to ranged actions while kneeling).

Leap: The distance a character may leap depends upon so many factors (level of gravity, an individual's encumbrance and fatigue, the nature of the surface being jumped from, the amount of headroom available, etc.) that GM determination by exact circumstances is essential. However, as a guideline, the following sample distances in normal gravity are provided.

Vertical Jump: Characters can jump from a standing position roughly one centimeter high per point of Fitness; double that if a character runs at least three meters prior to jumping.

Horizontal Jump: Characters may jump horizontally from a standing position roughly one meter plus an additional two centimeters per point of Fitness. For running broad jumps, add an additional meter per meter run, to a maximum of double a character's standing jump distance.

Go Prone: This may be a simple drop to the ground or a leap for cover. Prone characters are a bit more difficult to hit with ranged attacks: apply a penalty of –30 to an attacker's score.

Combat Modifiers

In the futuristic environment of the BUGHUNTERS™ game universe, weapons often have built-in aids that can modify the chance to hit with ranged attacks. Environmental conditions may affect that chance as well.

Computer Assisted Targeting (CAT): Virtually all ranged weapons can be built with the computer assisted targeting option, adding a +5% modifier to the character's attack score when firing with that weapon.

Gyrostabilization: A gyro unit helps steady a ranged weapon for greater accuracy. The gyrostabilization option for weapons gives firers a +5% modifier to their attack score; these units must be built into the weapon itself.

Variant Gravity Situations: High and low gravity can modify Reflexes and Fitness checks unless characters have special equipment or the necessary skills to avoid these adverse effects. Other effects of variant gravity—such as its effect on thrown weapon combat—are discussed in the relevant sections of the rules.

Range Modifiers: Many of the weapons of the BUGHUNTERS game universe have fairly sophisticated ranging technology attached, but some still leave range adjustment to the unaided human eye. Use these attack modifiers in play:

Range	Unaided	Aided
Point blank	+10%	+20%
Short	—	+5%
Medium	–5%	—
Long	–15%	–5%
Extreme	–30%	–15%

Sighting Range: Sighting range is 50 meters for the unaided eye, but few UTRPF eyes go unaided. Vision enhancement equipment is common on military firearms, increasing sighting range to 150 meters. Enhanced sighting allows vital and non-vital targeting within that range.

Recoil: Slug-throwing weapons have either light, standard, or heavy recoil, as indicated in Chapter 5: Equipment.

A character must have a Fitness score of 30 to ignore the effects of light recoil, a score of 45 to ignore standard recoil, and a score of 60 to ignore heavy recoil. A character whose Fitness score falls below these values suffers a –5% modifier on attack rolls for every 10 points (or

Chapter 4: Combat & Repair

fraction thereof) below the requisite minimum.

Example: Slim, with a Fitness of 32, picks up a fallen automatic shotgun, which has heavy recoil. His Fitness is 28 points below the minimum required to wield a heavy recoil weapon without penalty (60–32=28), so he suffers a –15% on his attack roll (2.8 rounded up = 3; 3x5%=15%) as the recoil bounces him off a wall.

Effects in Low Gravity: Slug-throwing weapons have just as much recoil in low gravity, where firers have less weight to hold themselves steady. Unless a character is wearing a low-G exoskeleton or has the Low-G Maneuver combat skill, the required Fitness scores become 50, 65, and 80 for light, standard, and heavy recoil, respectively, with the same modifiers. Characters lacking such special equipment or training must also make a separate Fitness check with each shot to avoid being knocked off their feet if their Fitness isn't enough to enable them to absorb the recoil. If Slim, for example, were in a low-gravity situation, he would be 48 points below the Fitness requirement for the weapon, giving him –25% on his chance to hit. Also, if he fails a separate Fitness check, firing the automatic shotgun will nearly launch him into low orbit.

Armor: The various armor types in the Equipment section list by how much they reduce both the damage done by a hit *and* the weapon's Lethality Rating. The armor shields its wearer from that amount of damage from every hit, even if hit more than once in a single turn. Armor tends to cover vital areas rather than non-vital ones, and this should be kept in mind when characters are targeting specific body parts.

Cover: In the BUGHUNTERS™ game, cover is divided into three categories: soft, hard, and impenetrable. Concealment by any type of cover causes a –5% to –80% chance to hit, depending on how much of the target body is so concealed. Determination of the exact modifier is left to the GM, based upon the circumstances at the time.

In the future environment of the game, *impenetrable* cover is just that: no weapons wielded by the characters will be able to pierce it. However, many types of merely *hard* cover can be "softened" with heavy weapons. Concrete or metal floors and walls, stone embankments, and other forms of cover may rate as hard at the beginning of a combat scene but subsequently be reduced to slag by repeated heavy weapons fire. The exact reduction is up to the GM, but what remains is either soft cover or nothing.

Impromptu Weapons: Some adventure scenarios will find humans and synths caught unawares, facing hordes of bugs without a single adequate weapon to be found. Under those circumstances, the tools at hand have to be fashioned into effective weapons.

For hand-to-hand combat, almost anything can serve as a club or, if jagged or sharpened, a knife or sword. The equipment charts on pages 126-127 list damage ratings for some common impromptu weapons.

Stun Pistols & Tranquilizers: These weapons are tuned to be effective against humans. As such, they are unpredictable when used against alien entities with completely different biologies. The children of other stars are as likely to be unaffected by these weapons as anything. When using stun pistols or tranquilizers against untried bugs, the effects are up to the GM. Possible results can range from ineffective to partially effective to the incredible and unexpected—increasing the bug's agility for a short time, for example.

Previously encountered bugs may have tranquilizers designed for them (at the GM's option, assuming that a proper lab receives a living specimen). If the proper round is loaded into the gun, a hit should have the desired effect.

Explosives

Damage from explosions consists of two different types. The first is caused by the concussive force, which affects everyone within its area but decreases rapidly with distance from the explo-

Chapter 4:
Combat & Repair

sion's center. The second is damage caused by flying fragments, which have a progressively lesser chance of hitting anyone as distance from the explosion increases but hit with roughly the same force regardless of that changing distance.

To represent this, explosives are listed with a damage code in the equipment chapter. The number before the first slash mark is the amount of concussive damage done to anyone within five meters of the explosion's center. Half that damage (round down) is done to anyone within ten meters, half that to anyone within fifteen, and so on, until the damage reaches zero points. The number in the middle is the chance of someone being hit by fragments within five meters of the explosion's center. Halve this percentage (round down) for those within ten meters of that center; halve it again for anyone within fifteen meters, and so on. The final number is the amount of damage done to anyone hit by fragments, regardless of the range.

Poisons

Some of the xenoforms PCs may encounter in the course of the game have venomous attacks. The following poison rule will help the GM judge the game results of such attacks.

Poison does damage not only when first injected into a victim but also for several rounds thereafter. To determine its exact effects, roll the appropriate damage and apply that for the first turn. Then, on each subsequent turn, the victim suffers further damage from poison in the system but at a cumulative −1 per round as the venom loses potency, finally stopping when the damage per round reaches zero.

For example, imagine that a PC injected with a poison rated at 2d6 initial damage suffers 8 points of damage the first turn. The unfortunate victim would suffer 7 more points on the second turn, then 6 on the third, and so on until the damage reached 0 on the eighth and final turn.

Coolness Checks

Some situations require characters to make a Willpower test to avoid reacting instinctively.

Autofire: Characters who become the target of autofire must make a check to avoid going prone automatically. They make this check the instant they are fired at, and if it is failed, they immediately go prone, even though it is not currently their turn to act.

Characters who wish to enter an area of autofire must pass a Willpower test to do so. If it fails, they may not enter the area but may otherwise take their turn as normal.

Horrific Sight: The GM may require a Willpower test at any time, with any modifiers desired, to determine if a character freezes or flees when faced with a horrifying sight of some sort. This test may use failure margin ratings (as set by the GM) to differentiate between panicked flight and petrifying fear.

Chapter 4: Combat & Repair

For example, a GM might ask a player to make a Willpower test when that player's character sees a companion torn to pieces by an alien monstrosity. If the test fails, the GM might rule that the character flees out of danger; if the failure margin is exceeded, the ruling might be that the character instead freezes in panic.

The GM should note that civilians and rookies should be subject to such checks more often than veteran UTRPF troopers.

Vehicles in Combat

Combat in BUGHUNTERS™ adventures generally involves ground maneuvers by limited numbers of characters. For that reason, considerable detail is given to hand-to-hand and Small Arms fire combat. When vehicles are present, the focus will still typically be on hand-to-hand fighting and Small Arms fire, with the vehicle being treated as cover (something like a mobile building). This focus on individual combat is only natural, given the theme of the game, in which individual characters perform heroic actions while face-to-face with hideous creatures. Occasionally, however, GMs may desire to run larger or more complicated combats involving vehicles.

In either case, GMs may decide to use the additional combat rules that follow. Note, however, that the focus of such combats should be on dramatic development of the story, and conflict should return to the personal level as soon as possible.

Surface Combat

GMs should characterize each vehicle's movement in combat as the equivalent of a type of foot movement. "Walk" means the vehicle is traveling slowly (though still faster than a normal human walk, usually). "Run" means that the vehicle is traveling at its normal cruising speed; this normally requires a road or other smooth surface for ground vehicles—a grassy meadow *may* be smooth enough, but a rocky field will likely not be: the GM should decide based upon the vehicle's ruggedness and the exact type of field. "Sprint" means that the vehicle is travelling at or near top speed, which typically requires a well-kept road.

Where planetary atmospheres permit, helicopters and other VTOL (vertical take-off and landing) vehicles may move at any of these rates. They usually needn't worry about ground conditions (air conditions, however, may be another story . . .). Other aircraft may move no slower than a run; many no slower than a sprint.

With these movement rates in mind, apply the normal combat rules to the actions of characters riding such vehicles. The GM may allow bonuses to rolls against large targets such as vehicles and buildings or for sophisticated targeting equipment and computer programs built into a vehicle.

For shots versus vehicles, GMs may assign a number of hit points and armor ratings to a target and then use the normal rules for damage. Stamina damage reflects relatively superficial injury that may accumulate to serious levels; body damage reflects hits on essential systems such as engines, and GMs are encouraged to turn these into story elements, applying appropriate speed penalties, etc.

Aerospace Combat

The high speeds, durable materials, and heavy weaponry of air and space combat vehicles makes combat between such vehicles even more problematical. Nonetheless, the following abstract system will provide for role-playing needs.

Getting Started: Determine the number of ships in the conflict. Ideally, there should be only two: the UTRPF ship and the enemy ship, but sometimes more ships will be present. Note the number of laser mounts and how many missiles each ship has.

Alien Weaponry: Some aliens may have

Chapter 4:
Combat & Repair

weapon systems that are beyond human science. These weapons may be the equivalent of lasers or missiles; if so, treat them as such and continue. Other alien weapons, energy dampers, or force fields must be dealt with purely by role-playing. Super-scientific weapons that render human ships helpless are the very stuff of science fiction. Don't be afraid to use them if it creates an epic shipboard struggle between troopers and bugs.

The Round: Each round is some length of time appropriate to the story. If a fast combat is desired, each round can represent 10 minutes. If a drawn out action is desired (in order to build suspense and isolation), each round can represent an hour or more. In each case, the time used is up to the GM.

Combat: During the round, it is assumed that all lasers are firing as the ships maneuver in and out of range. Also, ships can fire one of their missiles at each other every round, but once expended, these cannot be replaced. In general, weapon systems are very sophisticated and deadly, but the tremendous distances involved, complicated by the nature of the Isler Drive or sub-light vector movement, make it difficult to score a hit, requiring a successful roll versus the Gunnery skill to do so.

Damage: Roll 1d6 on this table for every hit achieved. If the target does not possess the item rolled, treat the shot as a glancing hit that produced no serious damage.

1. Laser mount destroyed
2. Missile launcher destroyed
3. Drive disabled
4. Power source disabled
5. Module destroyed
6. Module destroyed

Laser Mount Destroyed: One of the ship's laser mounts is scrubbed from the ship, leaving a charred scar on the hull.

Missile Launcher Destroyed: The launching bay for the ship's missiles is severely damaged,

making it impossible to fire more missiles. Also, 1d6 remaining missiles are destroyed in the explosion.

Drive Disabled: The ship's propulsion unit is knocked out, leaving it stranded in deep space. It's only a matter of time before the other ship matches courses and the boarding begins.

Power Plant Disabled: The ship's power generation systems are rubbled. Emergency battery power keeps life support going, but no other shipboard equipment will function. With no power, the drives are also disabled, as described above.

Module Destroyed: One of the ship's modules is gutted. There are five types of modules: Bridge, Sleeper, Crew, Transport, and Drive. Randomly determine which type is hit. All equipment in the affected module is destroyed, with no opportunity of repair. Personnel there are killed, unless they are already wearing space suits and pass a Reflexes test to avoid having their suits holed.

Resolution: This system does not allow for total ship destruction with lasers or missiles. Some sort of hulk will be left, which can be boarded.

Ships can be repaired, but not in the scope of a game. If a damaged ship can be towed to a space dock, long-term repairs can be implemented, taking weeks or months to complete.

Repair

Once damaged in combat, personnel can be repaired.

Healing: Unaided healing occurs just as described in the AMAZING ENGINE™ rules, at the rate of one body point per week and 1d10 stamina points per 8 hours of complete rest. This rate can be accelerated by use of drugs or other treatments.

First Aid/Emergency Medicine: A successful First Aid or Emergency Medicine roll restores 1d6 stamina points **or** 1 body point. If the treater has a medkit or doctor's kit available, a successful roll restores 2d4 stamina points **or** 2 body points. If the Emergency Medicine skill is being used in a fully equipped sick bay or hospital emergency room, 2d6 stamina points **or** 4 body points can be restored. The GM may allow aid to be performed more than once on the same victim's wounds in order to attempt to restore both stamina and body points. The GM may also allow subsequent rolls by characters with higher skill and/or better equipment, to attempt a more favorable result (such as a physician with a doctor's kit retreating a wound that has been treated previously by a field medic). **The results in such cases are not cumulative; rather, only the most favorable one is used.**

Stimulants: Injected stimulants only restore stamina points. Once taken, the stimulants create a pool of additional stamina points to keep the character moving, but only temporarily, and only at the cost of body points, as indicated in the table below. Once the time period is up, the character loses the artificially gained stamina points.

Stimulants can bring an unconscious character around, provided the stamina generated brings the total to greater than zero. Coming down from the stimulants can cause a character to become unconscious if the total at that time plunges below zero.

There are a wide variety of stimulant drugs available, from different manufacturers, with different dosages. However, they can all be divided into these three categories:

Type	Stamina Restored	Duration	Cost in Body pts
Light	15 points	1 hr	1
Medium	30 points	2 hr	2
Heavy	90 points	3 hr	4

Hospitalization: Hospitalization can affect both stamina and body points. Hospitalization requires immobility as various devices and personnel administer treatments. Every hour in such hospitalization heals 1d4 stamina points. Each

consecutive eight hours also heals one body point.

Regrowth: Extreme body damage can be cured with regrowth. New limbs and body parts can be cloned and force-grown in a matter of a few weeks, but only with the right equipment, as indicated in the equipment chapter.

Even a character who is technically dead (i.e., one who has been reduced to zero body points) can be brought back to life, provided the brain was not severely damaged and what remains of the character is placed in a stasis pod within five minutes of "death." Upon return to Stargate, such a character is attended by experts who force-grow replacement body parts. However, the afflicted character must pass a Fitness check to survive revival from stasis.

Brain Damage (Optional Rule): As GM, you may, if you desire, allow revival of characters that have been at zero body points for a period longer than five minutes. However, after five minutes without normal blood circulation, the human brain has a high risk of permanent damage. To represent this, have the "dead" character make two Fitness checks, each with a penalty of –5 per minute beyond the initial five minute "window." If the first test is passed, the character's breathing and circulation is restored (otherwise the character is irretrievably dead). A revived character who passes the second test suffers no permanent brain damage; but if this second test is unsuccessful, the character loses points from both Intuition and Learning equal to the amount by which the test is failed. Players whose PCs suffer severe brain damage should be allowed to retire them and create new ones.

Example: Jackson has a Fit of 56 and has been at zero body points for 7 minutes before being placed in a stasis pod. For purposes of the revival tests, his Fitness of 56 is penalized –10 (7–5=2; 2x5=10), yielding a 46. He barely passes the first test with a roll of 45. But he misses the second with a roll of 52, and loses 6 points (52–46) from both Lea and Int.

Chapter 5: Equipment

"The object of this exercise is to familiarize you with the array of standard weapons available to you as troops of the United Terra Reconnaissance and Peacekeeping Force.

"All these items should be used with the following strategy in mind: the point is not to die for your planet. Instead it is to make sure the motherless creatures you'll be facing die for their planet. No offense intended.

"This strategy depends upon judicious usage of the devices you see before you."

—Drill Sergeant Jack Rasiko, UTRPF

Explanation of Terms

The equipment in this chapter is divided into general headings by availability to synners. Under each heading, the items are listed in a rough order from smaller to larger. Each item includes a list of salient statistics; those subheadings are explained as follows.

Cost: This is the typical price a synner would pay to acquire the equipment for private possession. It reflects a number of factors, including availability of the item and legality of private ownership of it. GMs are free to adjust these prices as they see fit, to suit individual situations. *Note that UTRPF troops do* not *have to pay for weapons assigned to them.*

Weight: This is the weapon's weight when fully loaded.

Mag.: This is simply a listing of how much ammunition a weapon's magazine will hold. **Once the magazine is empty it must be replaced before the weapon can be fired again.** Such reloading typically takes one turn for Small Arms; twice that for Heavy Weapons.

ROF: An abbreviation for **R**ate **o**f **F**ire, this heading lists how fast a weapon can put out rounds. In the case of weapons that can do single shots, bursts, *and* fully automatic fire (autofire), several numbers are listed. The first is how many single shots the weapon can fire in a combat turn (snapfire). The second is how many

rounds of ammunition are expended in a burst. Since a weapon may fire as many bursts per round as it can single shots, multiply this by the number of bursts fired to determine how much ammunition is expended. The third is how many rounds are expended in a turn for autofire.

Damage: This is a listing of how many points of damage the weapon causes. For hand-to-hand weapons, a separate listing may be given for melee combat as opposed to damage done by the weapon if thrown. For firearms, the listing is the damage per single shot. A burst does double this damage and increases the lethality rating by one; autofire quadruples the damage and increases the lethality rating by 3. For explosives, the first notation is the amount of damage done by concussion, the second the percentage chance of hits from fragmentation, and the third the damage done by each piece of shrapnel which hits. Shaped charges have a separate listing for front as opposed to sides and rear. Each of the four directions—front, left, rear, and right—is considered a 90° arc. Other weapons with special effects will have them listed in their descriptions.

Range: The range for thrown objects depends upon the thrower's Fitness, as explained in the combat chapter (p. 49). For direct-fire ranged weapons, the listing is the distance in meters for short, medium, and long range, in that order. Point-blank range for all such weapons is three meters. Indirect fire weapons (e.g., mortars) work differently and have only a single range listed.

Recoil: This heading is included on all hand-held ranged-fire weapons and identifies whether the weapon is considered light, standard, or heavy in terms of its "kick" when fired. For the effects of these recoil ratings, see pages 51-52.

Standard UTRPF-Issue Weapons

UTRPF has a variety of items that are considered standard issue equipment for missions. This

Chapter 5: Equipment

is not to say that all of these items are assigned for each and every mission, however. Rather, the exact equipment issued depends upon the perceived threat level of the mission. On the one hand, UTRPF HQ wants to make certain that its troops are adequately equipped before it sends them into combat. On the other, it is hesitant to turn synners loose with more weaponry than they really need at the moment, lest they prove their detractors right and lead some sort of armed revolt against humanity.

As a consequence of these two conflicting worries, synners sometimes find themselves somewhat over-equipped for a mission. More often, they find themselves slightly underprovisioned, particularly in terms of ammunition—and the best firearm in creation is of little use when it's empty of ammo.

Combat Knife/Bayonet

This hand-held item is made of a single piece of high density ceramic, the forward edge of which is fitted with a titanium blade. This cutting edge allows the knife to slice through even combat armor with relative ease. Sharp-edged hyper-carbon crystals stud the rear edge of the knife, creating a sawblade that is also a handy trench fighting weapon. It is balanced for throwing, and its hollow handle can hold a variety of items from a survival kit to a doctored high explosive round.

Cost: $45; Weight: Negligible; Damage (hand-to-hand): 1d6(3); Ranged Damage: 1d4(3)

Stun Pistol

This hand-held weapon is designed to function in a similar fashion to the tasers of 20th-century Earth, with two major differences. First, the stun pistol is built to carry multiple rounds, like a more typical firearm; second, its rounds are completely wireless. The pistol fires a self-contained, electrically charged round that, unlike those of tasers, emits electricity at the precise voltage necessary to bring down its victim. These rounds cannot be fired by any other weapon.

There are three settings:

Small: damage 1d10(0)
Human-sized: damage 2d10(1)
Large: damage 4d10(2)

Before firing, the trooper sets the toggle to the appropriate setting. Circuitry inside the gun proper sends coded impulses to the microchip in each ammo round. The software in the round then charges to release the appropriate voltage. The setting can be changed between firings.

Note that stamina points lost as a result of stun round damage return much more quickly than other damage and should be kept track of separately. Each 1d6 minutes, one such stamina point is recovered. On the other hand, body damage caused by stun rounds is recovered at the normal healing rates.

Cost: $300, plus $10 per round; Weight: 0.5 kg; Mag.: 13; ROF: 3; Damage: see above; Range: 15/30/50; Recoil: Light

Heavy Pistol

This semi-automatic handgun is similar in size and shape to the 50-caliber "Desert Eagle" popularized in late 20th-century cinema. Since it fires such an enormous round, it takes a variety of specialized ammunition. Some types are listed below, with clip capacity, damage, and ranges for each. Note that in each case, the pistol can fire up to three rounds per turn.

Cost: $1200; Weight: 1.5 kg

Standard/Tracer: This non-propelled ammunition can be acquired either as normal rounds or as tracer rounds. The tracer burns with a colored flame as it streaks through an atmosphere. While capable of inflicting a fair amount of damage, it is primarily used as a flare.

Cost: $10 per round; Mag.: 13; ROF: 3; Damage: 1d10(4); Range: 20/40/60; Recoil: Heavy

Splatter: Similar to the X-notched bullets of the 20th century, this round is made up of an

Chapter 5: Equipment

impact-triggered memory plastic, set to shatter into a star shape to maximize damage. A small target will often disintegrate as a result, while a human-sized target might well lose a limb.

Cost: $25 per round; Mag.: 12; ROF: 3; Damage: 2d10(7); Range: 20/40/60; Recoil: Heavy

HEJA round: The **H**igh-**E**xplosive **J**et-**A**ssisted round, unlike other bullets, speeds up once it leaves the muzzle, due to the micro-ramjet incorporated into its construction. Its high velocity and explosive head make it the bane of armored opponents (manufactured or natural). This round is also known as a shrieker, thanks to the peculiar noise made by the tiny jet engine.

Cost: Not available; Mag.: 7; ROF: 3; Damage: 3d10(7); Range: 30/60/100; Recoil: Heavy

Tranquilizer Rifle

This gas-powered rifle is similar to those used by paintball warriors of two centuries ago. Instead of firing a dye-filled pellet, however, it is structured to fire a dart containing a pre-measured amount of a fast-acting, broad-spectrum tranquilizer drug which will render a human-sized target of roughly Terran biology unconscious for 1-5 hours.

Cost: $1500, plus $8 per round; Weight: 3.5 kg; Mag.: 30; ROF: 5; Damage: Tranquilize (see above); Range: 40/100/200; Recoil: Light

Assault Rifle

This weapon is the workhorse of UTRPF. It fires a 10mm caseless flechette round, with an autofire rate of 150 rounds per minute. Its light weight (4.5 kg loaded) and efficient design (with the magazine in the rear of the weapon) make it easy to wield accurately in any situation. Its snail shell magazine holds 200 rounds. An assault rifle can be fitted with a CAT scope to improve chances of hitting a target (see page 66). Bayonets, grenade launchers, and other devices are also easily mounted on this weapon.

Cost: $3000, plus $12 per round; Weight: 4.5 kg; Mag.: 200; ROF: 5/x8/25; Damage: 1d12(6); Range: 50/150/250; Recoil: Standard

Automatic Shotgun

Similar to the street-sweepers of days gone by, these weapons are made for one purpose: mayhem at close range. Unlike those earlier weapons, 22nd-century models have magazines and barrels made as disposable units (commonly known as fife and drums). This is because the heat of rapid fire tends to deform the barrels, rendering them useless after about 30 shots. These barrel clips come in flechette, explosive, and armor-piercing (AP) varieties. The popular term for this weapon is the Flyswatter.

Cost: $2400; Weight: 5 kg; Mag.: 30; ROF: 1/x8/15; Damage: see below; Range: 20/60/90; Recoil: Heavy

Flechette Round: Cost: $350 per barrel clip; Weight: 1.2 kg; Damage: 2d6(7)

Explosive Round: Cost: Not available; Weight: 1.4 kg; Damage: 3d8(8)

Armor-Piercing Round: Cost: Not available; Weight: 1.3 kg; Damage: 2d10(9)

Grenade Launcher

This unit is built to attach to the underside of the assault rifle. With the addition of an attachable stock, it also becomes an independent weapon. Intended to launch 40mm grenades in indirect fire, it can be pressed into direct fire in a pinch. Its magazine holds 15 rounds of any of five grenade types: flechette, fragmentary, incendiary, smoke, and stun.

Cost: $2600; Weight: 1.4 kg (2.6 with self stock); Mag.: 15; ROF: 1; Damage: See grenades; Range: 100/200/300 direct, 400 indirect; Recoil: Heavy

Chapter 5: Equipment

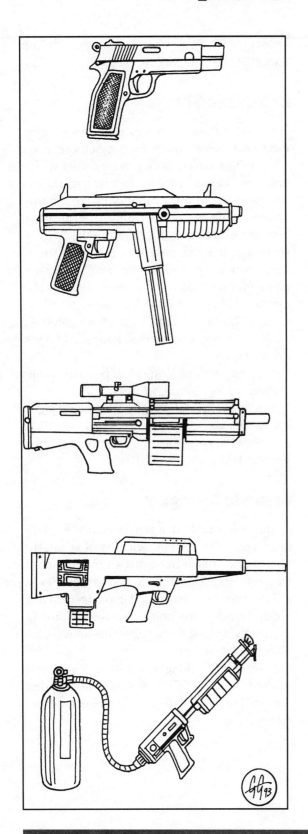

Small Mortar

This mortar is basically a bipod-mounted version of the grenade launcher, built for greater stability and rate of fire. It launches 40mm grenades (fragmentation, High-Explosive, incendiary, smoke, and stun) in indirect fire but cannot readily be used for direct fire. It has no magazine. Rather, each round is dropped into the barrel individually and launches when it strikes the firing pin at the bottom.

Cost: $4200; Weight: 15 kg; Mag.: 0; ROF: 2; Damage: See grenades; Range: 400 indirect

Flame Thrower

Unlike its bulky predecessor of WWII vintage, this is a self-contained unit that enables the wielder to act without being hampered by bulky tanks and hoses. Pressurized, self-contained tanks of "friendly napalm" eliminate the danger of being flambéd by one's own weapon if hit by enemy Small Arms fire: an electronic sparker at the weapon's muzzle converts the high velocity stream of an otherwise inert chemical compound into a flame hot enough to overload standard heat dispersion equipment and render even the toughest armor lethally hot in mere seconds.

Although the weapon does not fire rounds per se, the duration and coverage of its flaming stream can be simulated by treating it in the same manner as other ranged weapons, as indicated in the statistics that follow.

Cost: $3000, plus $120 per "round"; Weight: 22 kg; Mag: 10; ROF: 1/x5/10; Damage: 2d6(4)/turn; Range: 5/10/15; Recoil: Light

Howler Machine Gun

This semi-portable weapon weighs in at approximately 10 kg unloaded, with a barrel caliber of 25mm. Its six rotating barrels can fire chemically boosted, magnetically accelerated rounds at the rate of 2,500 a minute. The Howler can be mounted on a bipod or tripod, or it can

Chapter 5: Equipment

be fitted with hand grips for when combat gets up-close and personal.

The machine gun fires standard, tracer, splatter, HEJA (**H**igh-**E**xplosive **J**et-**A**ssisted), HEAP (**H**igh-**E**xplosive **A**rmor-**P**iercing), HFAT (**H**igh-**E**xplosive **A**nti-**T**ank), and UHDUG (**U**ltra **H**igh-**E**xplosive **D**epleted-**U**ranium, **G**uided) rounds.

The Howler is often used with CAT or a targeting visor for a bonus to attack rolls. Its backpack magazine holds 2,000 rounds, which can be mixed from the selection above.

Cost: Not available; Weight: 14.5 kg; Mag.: 2,000; ROF: 4/x50/500; Damage: see below; Range: 25/50/80 (HEJA: 35/70/100); Recoil: Heavy

Standard/Tracer: For autofire, tracer rounds are commonly added to standard ammunition (every fifth round being tracer) to assist a firer in adjusting fire (+5 to hit). Of course, this also makes the firer's position obvious to enemies.

Cost: $10 per round; Damage: 1d10(4)

Splatter: Cost: $25 per round; Damage: 2d10(7)

HEJA round: Cost: Not available; Damage: 3d10(7)

HEAP Rounds: Cost: Not available; Damage: 3d12(8)

HEAT Rounds: Cost: Not available; Damage: 4d10(9)

UHDUG Rounds: Cost: Not available; Damage: 4d12(9)

Laser Sniper Rifle

Unlike the projectile weapons that are standard UTRPF fare, lasers are fragile devices not suited for the rough-and-tumble lifestyle of the footsoldier. The bulky power units necessary to run them, coupled with their low ROF due to single shot lasing crystals, make them unsuitable for firefights. Furthermore, smoke, rain, and other such airborne particles diffuse a laser, reducing or even negating damage to its target. On the other hand, when conditions are right the searing heat delivered with each shot of a laser makes them excellent for situations where a one-round kill is needed.

The Deadeye sniper rifle has become infamous throughout the ranks of UTRPF, and its users are looked upon with respect and not a little trepidation. This is not due to the power of the weapon itself, which is formidable, nor to the ease with which they can conduct a line-of-sight kill, but rather the fiendish cleverness which these people display in ambushing their targets (sometimes even bouncing shots off mirrors!).

Cost: Not available; Weight: 7 kg; Mag: 10; ROF: 2; Damage: 3d10(6); Range: 100/250/400; Recoil: Light

Motion-Sensing Repeating Auto-Laser

This is a non-portable weapon primarily used for perimeter defense. Like the sniper's laser, it will not function well in hazy conditions. The Disco Light (as it is commonly called) is not remotely gun-shaped, although it is chain-fed, like an automatic gun. Instead of cartridges, the chain belt carries multiple lasing crystals that click into place and are cracked by the enormous energy surges sent through them. The weapon's vertical "barrel" terminates in a multi-faceted scintillator that splits each laser burst into myriad spears of light to perforate its targets at a maximum range of a full kilometer. The Gunnery skill of the person setting it up serves as the laser's fire accuracy.

Cost: Not available; Weight: 50 kg; Mag: 5,000; ROF: 2/x6/100; Damage: 4d10(6); Range: 200/500/1000

Portable Missile Launcher

This device is similar in design to the bazookas of WWII. However, there are three main differences. First, instead of being merely a pipe, the tube's rear is fitted with a series of vents that

Chapter 5: Equipment

channel the majority of the backblast upward and downward, using the remainder to operate the weapon's reloading mechanism. Second, instead of placing missiles individually into the launcher, the user loads a magazine that holds 10 shots. Third, each missile carries its own targeting computer and maneuvering jets to guide it to the target. The firer merely makes a Heavy Weapons skill test before firing to acquire target lock-on.

Cost: Not available; Weight: 30 kg; Mag: 10; ROF: 1; Damage: 20d10(9) (plus side/rear effects of satchel charge); Range: 200/500/2000; Recoil: Heavy

Standard-Issue Explosives

The explosives commonly issued for UTRPF missions fall into three divisions: hand grenades, launched grenades, and satchel charge.

Hand Grenades

Hand grenades come in the following four types; each treated as a 1 kg object for purposes of determining throwing range (see page 49).

Smoke: This grenade is used to generate smoke to limit visibility, hinder laser fire, or simply act as a signal. Its cloud covers a circle with a radius of five meters and lasts roughly two minutes (12 turns), though wind may narrow, lengthen, or disperse the cloud prematurely.

Cost: $10; Weight: 0.4 kg

Stun: Type I stuns by concussion. Cost: $15 per grenade; Weight: 0.3 kg; Damage: 16/—/—

Type II stuns by anaesthesia, requiring all unprotected creatures of roughly Terran physiology within its five meter cloud to pass a Fitness check or fall unconscious for 1d4 hours.

Cost: $20 per grenade; Weight: 0.4 kg

Fragmentation (Frag): The outer casing of this grenade is thick, hard metal or plastic which has been scored so that the internal pressure of the explosion breaks the casing into high-speed, sharp-edged fragments.

Cost: $30 per grenade; Weight: 0.4 kg; Damage: 16/80%/4d10(4)

Incendiary: White phosphorous, also known as WP or "willy-pete," is an incendiary device known for its anti-personnel applications. Once ignited, white phosphorous explodes into thousands of white-hot fragments that are self-relighting when exposed to air. These present a particular difficulty to medical personnel; removal of such a fragment from a victim is best done with the affected part(s) in an I-Chamber (see Medical Equipment).

Cost: $35 per grenade; Weight: 1 kg; Damage: 16/90%/2d12(4) (—/—/per turn)

Launched Grenades

Both the grenade launcher and mortar can launch versions of all four hand grenade types. Grenade launcher rounds cost double the price of a similar hand grenade and weigh 20% more; mortar rounds cost triple and weigh 40% more, the extra weight being propellant. In addition, the following two types of launched grenades exist which have no hand-delivered counterpart.

Grenade Launcher Flechette Round: This grenade is specially designed for those occasions where the grenade launcher is pressed into direct-fire duty as a shotgun.

Cost: $15 per round; Weight: Negligible; Damage: 2d8(7); Range: 25/70/100

HE Mortar Round: This High-Explosive round is tailored for indirect-fire mortar use.

Cost: $50; Weight: 1.5 kg; Damage: 24/90%/4d12(4)

Satchel Charge

This backpack-shaped chemical explosive device is used primarily for demolition (removing spaceship airlock doors, bringing down cavern roofs, etc.). On one side is a high-density ceramic plate which shapes the explosion. This plate can be removed to create a shapeless explosion.

Chapter 5: Equipment

The plate can also be removed and replaced with a fragmenting cover for use as an anti-personnel mine. Adhesive patches enable the satchel charge to cling to walls, floors, latrines, and the like—wherever demolition is desired.

Cost: Not available; Weight: 2 kg; Damage: 80/70%/10d10(8) shapeless; 200/90%/20d10(9) shaped front; 60/40%/5d10(5) shaped sides and rear.

Civilian/Paramilitary Weapons

Besides the UTRPF weapons above, there are, of course, numerous types of paramiliary weapons and some few civilian models as well. UTRPF troopers may encounter these in the hands of other people they meet or may have a chance to purchase some of them privately.

Small Pistol

This palm-sized, semi-automatic civilian weapon is easily concealed on one's person or in one's belongings. Useful only at close range, its light plastic construction and the availability of illegally constructed military-style rounds make it a favorite for firefights in close quarters where a larger weapon would be awkward. Many designer colors and patterns are available.

Cost: $275, plus $2 per round; Weight: 1 kg; Mag.: 4; ROF: 4; Damage: 1d6(3); Range: 10/20/40; Recoil: Light

Large Pistol

Weapons this size generally appeal to those more concerned with impressing others than actual firepower. Although the pistol is difficult to conceal because of its barrel length and caliber, the recent availability of black market jet-assisted (JA) rounds is causing a dramatic rise in the weapon's popularity.

Cost: $650; Weight: 1.5 kg
Standard Rounds: Cost: $5 per round; Mag.: 13; ROF: 3; Damage: 1d8(4); Range: 20/35/50; Recoil: Standard

JA Rounds: Cost: $25 per round; Mag.: 10; ROF: 3; Damage: 2d10(5); Range: 25/50/90; Recoil: Standard

Machine Pistol, Corporate

About the size of a 50-caliber Desert Eagle, this pistol can fire single shots or bursts or unload its entire magazine of 150 bullets in a single turn. It sports a military-class computerized smart sight, coupled with a combination gyrostabilization/ recoil-suppression unit. This enables the weapon to remain relatively stable even during autofire, resulting in slightly better accuracy (reducing the usual autofire penalty from −30 to −25). The full variety of rounds is unknown, due to corporate security measures, but typical stats follow.

Cost: $3900, plus $4 per round; Weight: 2 kg; Mag.: 150; ROF: 5/x12/150; Damage: 1d6(3); Range: 30/80/150; Recoil: Standard

Rifle, Civilian

Civilian rifles vary from single-shot, bolt-action antiques to the modern ultra-light, disposable Troubleshooters favored by criminal elements; most are semi-automatic in nature. Rifles can be equipped with a variety of sighting devices. The upper limit for civilians is the laser sight, but modern military targeting devices like the CAT can be purchased illegally. Average statistics for these weapons are as follows.

Cost: $1700, plus $6 per round; Weight: 3 kg; Mag.: 6; ROF: 2; Damage: 1d8(5); Range: 50/150/300; Recoil: Standard

Civilian Shotgun

Since "Street Sweeper" style semi- and full automatic shotguns were banned in the early 21st century, all that is legally available to civilians are single-shot, single- and double-barrel

Chapter 5: Equipment

weapons. Some are styled to look similar to the UTRPF weapons, but they are very expensive. Average stats are as follows.

Cost: $950, plus $12 per round; Weight: 4 kg; Mag.: 1-5; ROF: 2; Damage: 2d6(5); Range: 10/50/80; Recoil: Standard

Auto-Shotgun, Special Forces

This is a standard issue firearm for national police and other government forces. It has a lower ROF than the UTRPF shotgun and is therefore not equipped with disposable barrels. However, its quite respectable ROF, coupled with a variety of lethal standard issue rounds, make it the last word (so far) in the law enforcement arms race.

Cost: Not available; Weight: 4.5 kg; Mag.: 15; ROF: 1/x4/12; Damage: see below; Range: 15/60/90; Recoil: Heavy

Flechette Round Damage: 2d6(7)
Explosive Round Damage: 3d8(8)
Armor-Piercing Round Damage: 2d10(9)

Protective Gear

Whenever soldiers enter combat, there is the chance that they will take a hit. Though the armor and exoskeletons described here do not make that chance less likely, they do ensure that the trooper has a better chance of surviving the damage. Of course, not all protective gear involves combat. For that reason, environmental suits are also listed here.

Armor is less effective against hand-to-hand attacks than ranged fire. Such attacks halve its protection ratings for both damage and lethality (round down).

Helmet and Flak Vest

This lightweight combination gives some protection to its wearer's most vital areas without restricting mobility the way full body armor does. It reduces damage of attacks by 3 points and lowers lethality ratings by 2.

Cost: $1200; Weight: 6 kg

Body Armor

This is the standard battle-armor of every UTRPF soldier. Made from lightweight plastic, it reduces damage from ranged-fire attacks against its wearer by 6 points and lowers the lethality ratings by 4. Wearing body armor inflicts a penalty of –1 to all initiative rolls.

Cost: $2200; Weight: 24 kg

E-Suit

Environmental suits, or E-suits, are designed to protect a person in hazardous environments. The most common E-suit is intended for use in the vacuum of space and is therefore typically called a spacesuit. It has a durable outer coating and is specially designed to maintain internal air pressure and circulation, to moderate internal temperature, and to provide some protection against radiation. Other E-suits may forgo the temperature equipment or add anti-corrosive coatings or external armor plating, whichever is most suitable for their intended environment.

The standard E-suit (space suit) resists puncture and therefore acts as armor capable of reducing damage by 4 points and lethality by 2. Note, however, that damage beyond 4 points punctures the suit. The addition of armor plates raises the damage reduction to 10, lowers lethality by 4, and imposes a –1 penalty to initiative.

Cost: Not available; Weight: 20 kg (30 kg with armor plating)

High-G Exoskeleton

When soldiers are called to duty on a high-G world, the high-G exoskeleton is an invaluable piece of equipment. The exoskeleton resembles, and is designed along the lines of, heavy machinery. Slightly more than two meters tall, the exoskeleton is designed less for protection than

Chapter 5: Equipment

to enable the soldier to function effectively in high-G.

The suit's exterior is not quite human-looking, having a squat appearance that belies its height. This design lowers the center of gravity, making it harder for the exoskeleton to be knocked over. The oversized feet provide a good base, keeping the suit upright and balanced. The thickly-padded, form-fitting interior supports and cushions the body, while servomotors assist in movement. Additionally, an on-board diagnostic system automatically monitors blood pressure at various locations, adjusting the suit's inflatable lining to prevent the wearer's blood supply from pooling in the limbs and abdomen and causing diminished circulation to the brain.

The exoskeleton conveys an armor bonus that reduces damage by 10 and lethality by 5 while imposing an initiative penalty of –1. Armor plates can be bolted onto its outer skin to enhance this protection to 20 points of damage reduction and a lethality reduction of 8, but this raises the initiative penalty to –2 and tends to overbalance the whole structure. Any attacks that strike a suit this heavily armored require the wearer to pass a High-G Maneuver test or fall over. A second such test must be passed for the wearer to stand again.

Cost: Not available; Weight: Not applicable to user (200 kg dead weight; 300 kg with armor).

Low-G Exoskeleton

Considerably more frequent than missions involving high gravities are those involving low ones. In cases that require synners to conduct low-G combat maneuvers, a low-G exoskeleton can be of great aid. This exoskeleton is an open, form-fitting framework with a prehensile tail and hooks attached to the wrists and ankles. It is designed to keep soldiers from being moved in cases where they want to stay put.

The hooks are designed so that wearers can attach themselves to surfaces in low-G, to prevent knockback from weapon recoil. The pre-

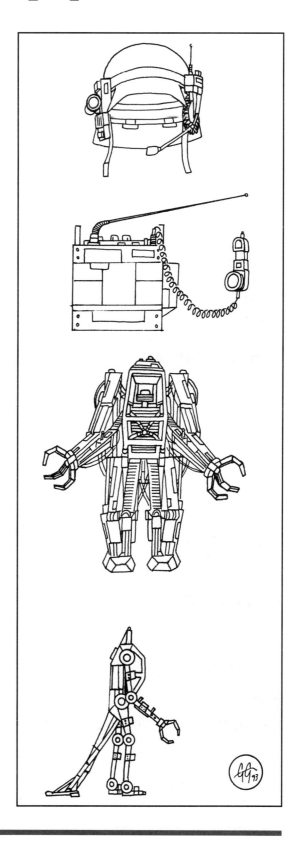

Chapter 5: Equipment

hensile tail, controlled by a plate inserted in the mouth, can wrap around poles to serve as an anchor of sorts or can stiffen to form the third leg of a tripod stance, thanks to a magnetic plate installed in the tip. Again, this aids a wearer to remain planted despite weapon recoil. Finally, the feet of the exoskeleton come equipped with magnetic plates (controlled by toe movement) to anchor the wearer to metal surfaces.

A specially-fitted combat armor suit can be strapped on over the exoskeleton, giving it the benefits and penalties listed for that suit, with the attendant benefits of the exoskeleton still applying. The low-G exoskeleton itself does not confer any armor bonus.

Cost: Not available; Weight: Not applicable to user (80 kg dead weight).

Reflective Armor

This shiny, flexible poncho is useful as a personal defense against laser fire, imposing a penalty of –10 to the laser's chance to hit. It also reduces the damage of successful laser attacks by 6 points and lowers their lethality rating by 4. Unfortunately, the poncho is both expensive and impossible to repair, and combat situations tend to tear and stain it into uselessness in short order.

Because of its reflectivity, the poncho is also effective protective gear in sunny environments.

Cost: $1500; Weight: 1 kg

Electronics

Weapons and armor are not, of course, the only things of use in UTRPF missions. The following electronic items can be helpful as well.

CAT (Computer Assisted Targeting)

This option can be built into any ranged fire weapon to add a +5 bonus to attacks. The cost is expressed as a percentage of the weapon's price.

Cost: +5 = 15%; Weight: 0.5 kg

Combat Radio

This backpack-borne radio serves as a combat unit's link to the outside, with a range of up to 120 km. Much more powerful than ordinary radios, it can cut through most shielding or jamming to transmit essential information or intelligence.

Cost: $1800; Weight: 4 kg

Engineer's Kit

This contains a set of basic electronic and mechanical tools for minor maintenance work and emergency repairs.

Cost: $200; Weight: 4 kg

Gyrostabilization

Like CAT, gyrostabilization can be built into any ranged fire weapon, adding a +5 bonus to chances to hit and costing a percentage of the weapon's normal price. The unit must be appropriate to the weapon's mass, so its weight is listed as a percentage of the weapon's loaded weight.

Cost: 10%; Weight: 25%

Helmet Array

Besides serving as an essential part of an UTRPF trooper's armor, this lightweight helmet also serves as a mount for equipment performing three other functions: communication, camera, and remote vital signs indicator. These three functions have a range of up to 7 km; in cases where there is no receiving base within that range, they can be routed through the nearest combat radio (see above).

The communicator, a small microphone, allows unit members to communicate with one another when outside of normal speaking range, as well as with their command post.

The camera allows commanders a remote glimpse at the action as it occurs.

Chapter 5: Equipment

The vital signs indicator reads the wearer's pulse, respiration, and brain wave activity. It can be fitted with stimulant auto-injectors (see Stimulants, page 56) to revitalize fallen troopers by radio command.

Cost: $600; Weight: Negligible

Holographic Recorder

This item has been perfected through years of redesign. One piece of "film" can hold multiple holograms, saving valuable storage space aboard tight ship quarters. Small nuclear batteries provide long-lasting power sources.

Cost: $40; Weight: 0.5 kg

Notepad Computer

Patterned after the stenographer's notepad of old, this interactive computer is about the same size as its predecessor (5" x 9"). It is made up of three parts: a detachable stylus, a stylo-pad, and an alpha-numeric keypad. Information can be entered in either of two ways: by writing on the stylo-pad with the stylus or by keying in data on the keypad. Sophisticated optical scanning enables the computer to read nearly any handwriting impressed on the stylo-pad in any known human alphabet. The stylus is also handy for entering data of a graphic nature, like design plans for ships, diagrams of attack sites, and drawings of xenoforms. The stylo-pad acts as a display screen whenever data is retrieved. Data can be downloaded into another computer for long-term storage. Notepads are handy when mission data needs to be recorded but voice transmission is prohibited and/or computer links are being monitored.

Cost: $300; Weight: 0.5 kg

Smartwear

This is a catch-all phrase for gear and clothing that adjusts to environmental needs (or personal preference, for the dilettante). Jumpsuits may be temperature-regulating; camouflage gear may change like a chameleon to match the surroundings; regulation clothes may become casual wear (shifting in style but maintaining the same mass as the original).

Smartwear is readily available in limited types to the general public. Military smartwear is more specialized and of course much more expensive. Rumors abound of new, experimental "shifter" smartwear covering the wearer from head to foot that can mimic xenoforms (within reason: no extra limbs or heads can be added, and body height/mass cannot be changed more than 10%).

Cost: $240; Weight: Negligible

Targeting Visor

The targeting visor plugs into the helmet; it can be raised or lowered as the wearer desires. These multipurpose visors come equipped with radar, sonar, telescopic sights, and spectrum-enhancing (infrared, low-light, or ultraviolet) settings which can provide a +5 targeting bonus, depending on conditions; if hooked into a CAT scope, the total bonus becomes +10. However, it is important to note that it will not identify non-moving targets as hostiles, nor those bearing transponders (e.g., a bug carrying a dead trooper): it only locks on to moving, non-UTRPF, targets.

Cost: $4500; Weight: Negligible

Transponder

This device serves to protect UTRPF soldiers from friendly fire. Built to clip on to soldiers' helmets, they can be easily removed if they ever become a detriment in combat—for example, if bugs begin to home in on the transponders'

Chapter 5: Equipment

transmissions. Any UTRPF computer targeting mechanisms automatically ignore any target bearing one of these gadgets. While this handy device has saved many a synner's life, some UTRPF officials fear the results if an enemy ever gets ahold of one.

Cost: Not available; Weight: Negligible

Medical Equipment

And, of course, various types of medical equipment are of great use in recovering from the wounds of combat missions.

Doctor's Kit

This kit contains roughly twice the equipment of a field medic's kit (see medkit, below), adding various scopes and gauges necessary for diagnostic procedures and including an array of common prescription drugs and intravenous fluids, as well as a basic set of surgery tools.

Cost: $300 (normally available to doctors only); Weight: 2.5 kg

I-Chamber

The isolation chamber is a small-to-medium-sized device used in surgical operations, especially those involving removal of white phosphorous grenade shrapnel from soldiers. It is filled with an inert gas, preventing the shrapnel from igniting on contact with air. I-chambers are made to fit limbs and torsos.

Cost: Not available; Weight: 15-60 kg

Medkit

This is the standard outfit issued to a marine field medic. It contains materials for the most commonly needed treatments—lotion for rashes, foot powder, adhesive bandages in a wide variety of sizes, antiseptic ointment, analgesic/anti-fever pills, antihistamines, antivenom injectors, etc. —as well as a small set of

surgical tools and plastic wound closures.

Cost: $125; Weight: 1.5 kg

Plugs

These cylinders are filled with various medical needs: adrenaline, antibiotics, sedatives, amphetamines, saline, Ringer's lactate, etc. They are needleless, self-contained injectors and are standard issue in UTRPF medical kits.

Cost: $45; Weight: Negligible

Portable Womb

This is a simpler but completely functional version of the full-size artificial wombs used in the cloning process. Made for field hospital use, a portable womb (or "oven") is used mainly for discrete body parts: arms, legs, fingers, toes, ears. Most field hospitals have ovens dedicated for specific limbs and organs.

Cost: Not available; Weight: 100-1500 kg

Synthetic Blood

This medical wonder was first developed in the early 1990's in response to fears of blood-borne diseases carried by tainted donors. Synthesized from bovine blood, this liquid needs no refrigeration (making it perfect for field hospitals) and acts as universal donor type O positive human blood. Each pint packet is vacuum-sealed, with a built-in universal adaptor for most standard sizes of medical tubing. Some less-sensitive medics refer to this life-saving fluid as "moo." Rumors are that other blood types (for xenoforms) are currently under development.

Cost: $600 per pint; Weight: 0.5 kg

Xenovax

Using a combination of genetic engineering and nanotechnology, chemists specializing in xenobiological diseases have created a group of human/clone vaccines, generically called xeno-

Chapter 5: Equipment

vaxes (for "xenobiological vaccines"). A single vaccine can be engineered to protect against specific diseases caused by a single xenobacteria or virus or against an entire category of diseases sharing common symptoms but with differing xenological origins.

For example, synners being sent to a planet known to harbor an alien bacteria or virus that cause diseases affecting the upper respiratory and nervous systems can be given a xenovax that will protect them against all known diseases caused by that alien "bug."

Xenovaxes cause a human body to synthesize materials not usually found in its normal state, at no risk to itself. Known poisons may be the key ingredient in a given xenovax; that 'vax will not only allow the body to create the poison but will change the body's chemical structure so that the poison does no harm to the host.

For long-term missions (several years or more) with known destinations, plugs (see above) with the appropriate xenovaxes are standard medical equipment.

Cost: Not available; Weight: Negligible

Vehicles

Besides spaceships (which are covered in their own chapter), synners sometimes need vehicles to get around in on the ground or in the air.

ATAPC

This tough ground car, commonly referred to as an ATAPC (**A**ll-**T**errain **A**rmored **P**ersonnel **C**arrier)—commonly pronounced "a-tapsy"—is the basic means of surface transportation for UTRPF troopers. Although it has wheels rather than treads and its primary purpose is transport not combat, it is still fairly formidable: the standard-issue vehicle has sufficient armor to stop natural attacks such as claws, horns, and teeth, as well as civilian Small Arms fire, and has gun mount hardware capable of mounting a repeating laser or missile launcher.

The interior of the vehicle has forward seats for a driver and a navigator and six seats in the passenger compartment. Driver and navigator each have a side hatch for entry; passengers enter through a wide rear hatch. In addition, there are three ceiling hatches: one above the navigator, to allow that individual to stand and operate as a gunner, and two in the passenger compartment, near the side gun mounts.

Top speed for the vehicle is 80 km per hour, and it can go for up to 72 hours before refueling.

Cost: Not available; Weight: 5 tons.

Hopper

The hopper is a two-person ultralight used for aerial reconnaissance, travel over rough terrain, and other quick, relatively short trips. It consists of an open framework with oppositely facing fore and aft seats and a power unit between them. In a vacuum, or for short hops in turbulent atmospheres, the vehicle is moved by lift jets mounted on stubby wings above the engine. These protuberances also serve double duty as mounts for twin propellers and as the sockets for glider wings when the vehicle is to be used in extended atmospheric flight.

Fuel consumption, and therefore flight duration, are highly dependent upon environmental conditions. As a rough guideline, the craft can maneuver in vacuum for 6 hours, fly in turbulent atmosphere for about 2 hours, and glide in calm air for 18 hours. Vehicle speed in each case remains roughly 50 km per hour.

Given its light weight, the hopper does not serve well as a gun mount (recoil is a problem), though its operators have an open field of fire and can attempt to use personal weapons.

Cost: Not available; Weight: 110 kg (with fuel).

Chapter 6: Ships

"None of these are sleek, streamlined ships like you'd see in those old movies. They're tight; they smell bad; and they don't always work the way they're supposed to. But jumping through hyperspace is a beautiful thing, and it's something no normal human will ever know."

—Star Lieutenant Alison Hawkins,
Hyperspace Pilot, UTRPF

Overview

Ships in the BUGHUNTERS™ universe are not very pretty, and they always look to be on the verge of falling apart. Nevertheless, they are functional and seldom fail in practice.

All UTRPF spacefaring vessels are modular in design. This allows fairly easy replacement when just part of a ship is damaged during a mission, and it allows comparatively quick assembly of just the right ship for the mission—in theory. In practice, standards are not always met, and a crew may be ordered to go on a long voyage with less than ideal facilities.

There are five types of modules used in ship construction: Bridge, Sleeper, Crew, Transport, and Drive. Several of these have more than one variation. To operate, a ship needs at least a Bridge unit and a Drive.

Module types are either stacked (meaning multiple units of that type may be used) or interchangeable (meaning only one type is used). For instance, only one Bridge unit will be used, but many Transport units can be attached to a large cargo hauler.

There are several standard ship configurations which will be discussed later. Standard missions include rescue, combat, reconnaissance, exploration, colonization, and delivery.

Layouts for module types and for several standard ships are shown later in this chapter.

Bridge Modules (interchangeable)

Bridge 1. Often called a two-seater, this module contains the minimum equipment needed to operate a ship. The two padded, reclining seats are used by pilot and navigator, and controls for most ship functions are easily accessible, including power, movement, weapons, communications, location, and navigation. This module is sometimes armed with a laser mount for defense. All ships must have at least Bridge 1.

A tight, one-person airlock uses most of the crawlspace beneath the module. A sliding trap door opens into it.

Mass: 15 tons.

Bridge 2. Commonly known as a four-seater, this module is Bridge 1 plus two extra seats and accompanying control panels. One of the extra panels holds duplicate controls for location and communications, while the other holds weapon controls. The seats are thus meant to be occupied by a radio operator and a gunner. Typically armed with two laser mounts, Bridge 2 is mandatory on exploratory, rescue, and minor combat missions; it is also the preferred bridge for colonization ships.

Mass: 25 tons.

Bridge 3. Known to troops as a shooter, Bridge 3 is simply Bridge 2 armed with four laser mounts and a bevy of six nuclear-tipped missiles. Ships on major combat missions must have Bridge 3, and it is preferred for all missions into known danger zones.

Mass: 35 tons.

Sleeper Modules (stacked)

Sleeper 1. This module contains minimal crew quarters, including a sink, sanitary facilities, and six equipment lockers. On each side of a central area, three sleeping areas are built into the bulkheads. Known as coffins because of their small, cramped design, each has a pull-down cover and room for a few personal effects. A small table can

Chapter 6: Ships

be pulled out from above each of the bottom beds, and six round seats can be pulled from the floor. On missions without Crew Modules, the central area of the Sleeper is used for meals (of reconstituted rations) and recreation. A narrow access corridor runs behind the coffins, and there are crawlspaces above and below the main unit.

Ships with more than four crewmembers, and ships on missions of more than 48 hours, must have at least one Sleeper module. More crew means more Sleepers, and as many as six can be stacked before it becomes more efficient to transport troops in stasis pods. Ships on long missions seldom stack more than four units, because the active crew of a ship rarely numbers more than 24, extra crew being kept in stasis.

For special occasions, such as the transport of a small number of human dignitaries, a Sleeper's bed units can be converted into stasis pods.

Stacked units are referred to as single modules, so four stacked Sleepers are a "Sleeper 4" rather than "four Sleepers."

Mass: 20 tons per unit.

Crew Modules (interchangeable)

Like Sleeper modules, all Crew modules have access corridors and upper and lower crawlspaces; they also have ports for extra weapons. Each Crew module's mess area is also used for meetings and briefings, and with the addition of a few terminals and screens can be made into a headquarters for ground operations.

Crew 1. This basic Crew Module contains minimal comfort facilities for a crew of up to 12 synths: a small galley, four shower units, a small clothes washer and dryer, and a mess hall. The table and bench chairs in the mess pull up from the floor, as do six small storage lockers in the galley. When the table and chairs are down, the central area can be used for exercise and recreation. Ships on missions expected to last more than seven days are required to carry at least a Crew 1.

Mass: 50 tons.

Crew 2. This extended Crew module is designed for up to 24 people, though 12 to 18 is optimum, and as many as 36 can use one in emergencies. A Crew 2 holds a small galley and a small sick bay with an attached lab and one convalescent bed which can be pulled up from the floor. Its expanded mess area has 10 small pull-up storage lockers, two pull-up tables, and 12 pull-up chairs. The chairs have folding backs, and thin pads stored underneath them can be flipped over the seat to provide some comfort. A Crew 2 also holds two locker rooms, each with three showers, 18 small lockers, and one clothes washer and dryer. Another washer and dryer combination is located between the locker rooms. The number of male and female synths on a mission is seldom equal, so one gender must sometimes double up for the sake of privacy.

A Crew 2 is officially required on missions of more than two weeks or any mission lasting more than one week and carrying more than two Sleepers, but in fact it is seldom used unless the mission is combat, rescue, or exploration.

Synth mission commanders can usually get human quartermasters to follow the regulations if they push hard enough and the module is actually available.

Mass: 80 tons.

Crew 3. This module, known to crews as the luxury liner, is very large and expensive.

A Crew 3 holds a brig with two small cells, an expanded galley, a large sick bay with four pull-up convalescent beds, and a separate lab. Four mobile chairs with magnetic lockdown are available for the lab and sick bay.

The mess area has the same fold-up chairs as in the Crew 2 and will hold up to 48 people for a meal. The chairs in this module can also be rotated (albeit only carefully and one at a time) to face in the same direction, making the area more conducive to briefings and meetings. The floor of the mess area holds 50 pull-up storage lockers, and the bulkheads hold six sets of clothes washers and dryers. The two locker rooms are also expanded, each holding six

Chapter 6: Ships

showers and 36 lockers.

Between the locker rooms is a gym with four resistant-force workout machines. An actual recreation room, usually with four virtual reality pods, as well as games, cards, and other equipment, completes the Crew 3.

Ships on major rescue missions, missions of more than 30 days (e.g., any interstellar mission), or any mission lasting at least two weeks and carrying at least four Sleepers, must have a Crew 3. This regulation is usually followed, though shortages sometimes result in a few long missions leaving port with only a Crew 2.

Mass: 130 tons.

Transport Modules (stacked)

Like other modules, each of these units has narrow access corridors and upper and lower crawlspaces.

Transport 1. This module, often referred to as a basket, is used to transport various small goods, such as seeds, some foodstuffs, raw materials, small equipment, and so forth. Combat ships almost always have a basket of ordnance of various types, as well as replacement parts and other materials. Shelves are sometimes installed, but crates are often simply stacked and secured with lines or nets.

Ships on delivery or combat missions and ships on very long missions need at least one Transport 1.

Mass: 15 tons empty; roughly 60 tons loaded.

Transport 2. Known officially as a personnel carrier and unofficially as a meatwagon, this unit carries stasis pods. Up to 100 pods can be stacked into the module. Pods plug into the module's forward bulkhead, and control panels can selectively end stasis for a given pod or set of pods. On some occasions, pods are filled with perishable food or medicine rather than people. When less than 100 pods are used, other goods are sometimes stacked in the remaining space, though this is technically a violation of regulations.

Colonization missions, rescue missions, and some delivery missions need at least one meatwagon.

Mass: 45 tons empty; roughly 170 tons loaded.

Transport 3. This module is an equipment carrier, known in some circles as a toybox. It is taller and wider than most other units, and it has five exits: its forward connection with the rest of the ship, the aft lock, huge port and starboard doors, and a ramp which lowers a large portion of the floor.

A Transport 3 is required on most exploratory, rescue, combat, and colonization missions, as well as some delivery missions. Almost anything can be hauled inside it, from ATAPCs and small spacecraft to tractors and cranes. In addition, a Transport 3 usually carries numerous heavy moving machines, as well as any building and repair supplies which might be deemed necessary. Large storage lockers can be raised from the floor, while most moving equipment is stored in bulkhead or ceiling bays until needed.

The lower crawlspace of a Transport 3 also supports a scoop and claw which can bring space debris into the hold. This involves an airlock which can be used by one person in emergencies.

Mass: 130 tons empty; roughly 2.5 kilotons loaded.

Drive Modules (interchangeable)

Drive 1. This module, the minimum needed for an UTRPF ship to operate in space, is attached to the rear of a ship. It includes an airlock unit capable of cycling four suited crew members at one time. Two large power units are attached to the airlock, one on the port side and the other on the starboard side.

Each power unit carries a small fusion reactor, shielding, and a supply of purified ice which is used for fuel for the fusion reactor. A ship going on a long journey often carries extra water in a cargo bay and in emergencies is capable of puri-

Chapter 6: Ships

fying water from ice found in space.

Behind each power unit is a small access corridor which can be entered from the module just forward of the Drive module. Crewmembers can enter the power unit's upper crawlspace from the access corridor or from the airlock. Most repairs can be made from the access corridor or crawlspace. Extra purified ice or water can be added to the reactor supply from the access corridor, which also holds manual controls for each power unit.

Using the manual controls is dangerous; the heat, radiation, and thrust is quite likely to kill anyone starting a power unit manually (consider the Drive to have a combat skill of 90, causing 3d6 damage with a lethality rating of 2, plus 3d6 damage with a lethality rating of 6). In addition, port and starboard engines must be started at the same time, or the ship will enter a spin.

A Drive 1 provides fair power, as well as good maneuverability for small ships (larger ships have very low maneuverability with just Drive 1). Ships with only a Bridge module or only Bridge and Sleeper modules are restricted to Drive 1.

Mass: 80 tons.

Drive 2. This module is a Drive 1 unit with two more aft power units, one port and one starboard. A ship must have a Crew or Transport module to accomodate a Drive 2.

Mass: 145 tons.

Drive 3. This module is a Drive 2 unit with two more aft power units, one port and one starboard. To support a Drive 3, a ship must have a Crew 3 module or a Transport 2 or 3.

Mass: 210 tons.

Drive J. This module adds Isler Drive jump units to a numbered Drive unit. The complete Drive module is referred to by its normal number, plus an indicator of the number of Isler units added, so a Drive 2 plus two Drive J units is called a Drive 2J2.

Each Isler Drive unit is a large sphere which is attached to the center of a normal power unit's top surface. A single power unit can thus support one Drive J unit, so a Drive 1 (with two linked units) can support two J units. Because of the requirements of balancing Isler jump fields, Drive J must always be used in pairs. Normally, a numbered Drive would support its maximum number of J units, so Drive 1J2, Drive 2J4, and Drive 3J6 are the most common. However, it is possible to operate with fewer than maximum J units, so Drives 2J2, 3J2, and 3J4 are also viable options.

It is also possible to overburden the power units by adding pairs of J units on the bottom of the Drive. However, it increases the side effects of the Isler Drive, especially when used with small ships. In addition, it may add a chance for the ship to become lost in hyperspace (see the sections on ship speeds and effects of the Isler Drive for more information).

Though potentially dangerous, extra J units are sometimes added to Drives which have been fine-tuned, increasing their power output enough to support extra J units. Rescue ships in particular are sometimes equipped with extra J units, because the benefits of extra speed outweighs potential dangers. A Drive 3 with eight J units is called a Drive 3J44, and has the J units equally spaced, with four above and four below. By the same token, a Drive 3J66 would have six above and six below, again equally spaced.

Drive J is necessary to travel interstellar distances.

Mass: 0.5 tons per unit (1 ton per pair).

Optional Accessories (added)

Option 1. This option adds extra weapons at strategic locations on the ship, with controls added on the Bridge. Standard additions with this option include automatic Anti-Craft Batteries, or ACBs. These may be set in three ways: to fire on all other craft; to track all other craft and offer the gunner the option to fire; or to not fire. ACBs can be placed anywhere on the ship's hull.

Another standard addition with Option 1 is a Chaff Launcher. This device may be added anywhere on the ship. It fires small missiles which

Chapter 6: Ships

detonate to release radar-fouling chaff, reducing by 80% the enemy's chance to hit with radar-guided missiles.

Other heavy weapons may be added to ships with Crew modules, because those modules have ports to support extra weapons. Option 1 is required on combat missions and encouraged on rescue and exploration missions.

Mass: 5 tons.

Option 2. This option adds additional maneuvering thrusters to a ship, with the number determined by the size of the ship and the desires of the pilot. Control is wired into the Bridge module.

Mass: 15 tons.

Option 3. This option adds various stealth aids. It includes coloring the ship a flat black to give it a low albedo, enabling it to shut off running lights, equipping it with radar jamming devices, and the like. Actual effects are left to the GM.

Mass: Minimal.

Standard Gear

Some standard equipment is included on all ships, regardless of size or shape. This includes landing gear, gravity generators, shields, and sensing devices.

The amount of landing gear is determined by the size and type of ship. It is retractable and is built into the crawlspace beneath each module. Bridge 1 modules have three small pads, while larger modules have more. All landing gear is controlled from the Bridge, though it may be controlled manually from the crawlspace as a back-up.

Launch rockets are also placed along the bottom of the ship. These lift the ship vertically, allowing its aft drive to power the ship into take-off and launch.

Gravity generators are also built into each module. They are redundantly configured and relatively failsafe unless utterly destroyed.

External sensors include cameras, radar, microphones (for operating within an atmosphere), and detectors for most forms of electromagnetic radiation.

Ship Assembly

When ship modules are put together, many links are forged: water and air circulation, electricity, and physical fastenings. This is not a trivial task, so despite the convenience of the modular design, ships are seldom rearranged once they have been built. Controls of most operations are wired into the Bridge module, but many pieces of equipment have local manual controls.

J Speeds

A ship's faster-than-light speed is measured by Jumps: Jump 1 means one second to charge the engines enough to move one kiloton one light second; this is equal to light speed. At Jump 10, it takes one second to charge the Isler Drive to move one kiloton 10 light-seconds—or 10 kilotons one light-second, or two kilotons five light-seconds, etc. While the charging time is a fixed amount, distance and mass moved are changeable, the one decreasing when the other increases and vice versa.

A ship's J speed is directly related to the number of Drive J units it carries. A ship weighing one kiloton and carrying two J units moves at Jump 2. A ship's actual maximum interstellar speed (light-seconds per second) is determined by dividing its number of J units by its mass in kilotons.

Ship Speed Examples

Ship	Mass	J Units	Speed
Combat Lander	3	12	4
Unloaded	0.65	12	18.5
Rescue Lander	3.1	12	3.9
Unloaded	0.576	12	20.8
Space Battleship	0.45	8	17.8
System Cruiser	0.34	2	5.9
Explorer	0.47	6	12.8
Colonizer	3.1	6	1.9
Unloaded	0.56	6	10.7
Fighter/Courier	0.13	2	15.4
Emergency Courier	0.097	4	41.2

Chapter 6: Ships

Of course, these figures reflect a performance in deep space, far from any gravity wells. Planetary gravities greatly lessen the drive's effectiveness—the greater the force of gravity, the less effective the drive. At planetary surface gravities, the jump becomes microscopically small. It isn't until roughly the 0.1 G point (for Earth, roughly 20,000 km up; for Sol, roughly 11 million km out) that the jump distance becomes sufficient to overcome the effect of gravity. Thus, ships move out of a body's main gravitational influence before engaging the Isler Drive.

Interstellar Travel Times: To determine how long it takes for a ship to travel from one star to another, simply divide the distance travelled by the ship's calculated speed (as shown in the box on the preceding page) and the result will be how long the voyage requires. Whatever unit of distance you use (light years, light months, light days, light hours, etc.) will determine the unit of time of your answer (years, months, days, hours, etc., respectively).

Examples of Interstellar Travel Times

Suppose a ship configured as a fully loaded Combat Lander is traveling at speed 4 from Sol to Alpha Centauri. The distance is five light years, which we'll convert to light months: There are 12 months to the year, so 5 light years equals 60 light months. 60/4=15. Thus, the Combat Lander will reach Alpha Centauri in 15 months.

Now let's try slightly more difficult numbers (time to break out your calculator!). Let's imagine that UTRPF is sending a ship configured as an Explorer (speed 12.8) from Sol to Altair, which is 16 light years distant, and we want to know exactly how many days it will require. A year consists of 365.25 days; therefore 16 light years equals 5,844 light days (16x365.25). 5,844/12.8=456.5625, so the vessel will make the trip in a little over 456 days.

Actually, however, we needn't be so precise, as the stellar distances on the foldout Star Map are not *that* exact, and actual ship speeds vary slightly from vessel to vessel. We could have simply rounded the ship's speed up to 13 and estimated that it would take roughly 14-15 months to make the trip.

Effects of the Isler Drive

The Isler Drive, which made travel to other stars practical, allows faster-than-light travel, but without time distortion. It is a "jump" drive, allowing instantaneous displacement of a ship from one spatial location to another.

The Isler Drive makes a rapid succession of jumps. Someone watching a ship from nearby would see it disappear when the drive is engaged; to those watching from a distance, the ship would seem to travel in a dotted line, blinking into and out of existence. To those on the ship, space passes by in sort of a freeze-frame movie, with colorful distortions caused by the jump.

For inanimate objects, there are no unusual effects; the jump is made without building inertia, so the ship receives no additional stress. For most living beings, the Isler Drive causes several problems: terrible nausea, extreme disorientation, and sometimes insanity. These effects often last long after the individual leaves the Isler field.

Sleep, regular or drug-induced, lessens the effects, but does not eliminate them entirely; it is chancy for a normal human to try to sleep through an Isler jump. Only the stasis pod, itself an adaptation of Dr. Isler's theories, protects a normal human from the jump effects. All UTRPF clones are specifically modified and trained to be almost entirely immune to jump effects.

From time to time, however, nearly all synths suffer a minor queasiness; this has come to be called "jump flu." When a synth starts a jump trip, a Fitness check must be made, with a penalty equal to the ship's speed. If the check fails, the synth suffers mild queasiness and must

Chapter 6: Ships

make a second check. If this check fails, the synth becomes violently ill and must make a third check. If the third check fails, the synth develops a minor neurosis and must make another check. If this fourth and final check fails, the synth develops a psychosis and must be forcefully restrained for the duration of the voyage. At the end of the trip, the synth must make a successful Fitness check to throw off any effects of the Isler field.

Normal humans suffer more during a jump unless protected by stasis, making a Fitness check once per day of travel, with a penalty equal to twice the ship's speed.

There is one other potential problem with the Isler Drive: the possibility of becoming lost in hyperspace. This phenomenon has been noted only in ships which have exceeded Jump 20. For game purposes, assume any ship travelling over Jump 20 has a percentage chance equal to the ship's speed of becoming permanently "stuck" in hyperspace. Because the chance of becoming stuck increases so dramatically above Jump 20 (from 0% at Jump 20 to 21% at Jump 21), Jump 20 has been declared the maximum safe speed for a starship. Regulations strictly prohibit the addition of enough Drive J units to cause a ship to exceed Jump 20.

Exactly what happens to such ships is presently unknown (i.e., in your GM's hands).

Standard Drive

The fusion drive units which provide a spaceship's main propulsion use simple action-reaction principles to achieve acceleration, and the standard rule of inertia applies: a motionless body requires energy to get it moving, and once it starts moving it tends to go in the same direction until another force acts to change its direction and speed.

In space, this means high-speed movie-style turns are virtually impossible, or at least inefficient. A ship wishing to reverse its present direction could travel through a graceful arc in order

to go the opposite way, but a realistic typical turn would go more like this: the ship begins by shutting off the aft drive. Still moving forward at the same speed, it uses maneuvering thrusters to rotate the ship. After a few seconds, maneuvering thrusters fire again to keep the ship from rotating too far, stopping it when it is facing the opposite direction from the direction of its travel. Finally the main aft thrusters fire again, first slowing the ship, briefly stopping its now backwards progress, and causing it to speed back the way it just came.

Loose items in the ship, including the crew, are affected by these forces, just as early astronauts were pressed into their chairs by the force of take-off. The ship's artificial gravity generators mitigate this effect somewhat, but it is still difficult for the crew to walk or move normally during take-off and maneuvers.

It should be obvious from the above that piloting and navigation in space are not easy matters. Travel times from one locale to another are dependent upon multiple factors, with distance, mass, and thrust being of primary importance. Point of origin and destination are never truly fixed locations; satellites orbit planets, which orbit stars, which are themselves in motion. The course of a vessel among these moving bodies also depends upon its mass, its thrust, and how long that thrust is applied.

In real life, calculating such things requires sophisticated mathematical formulas and is typically done by computer. In BUGHUNTERS™ adventures, such details of space travel will be left to the GM. But in general, you can trust that a vessel with a higher thrust-to-mass ratio moves faster than one with a lower such ratio and would generally be able to catch it, given enough time to match vectors and assuming it remained within sensor range during the interim.

Interplanetary Travel Times: Because the Isler Drive is functionable until within the 0.1 G range of a body's gravity well, travel between planets within the same system is typically a matter of mere hours or days, and travel between

Chapter 6: Ships

bodies as close together as the Earth and Moon requires merely a few seconds . . . except for two problems. First, jump speeds have to be reduced in high traffic areas: keeping track of multitudinous ship courses and adjusting for possible collisions requires a bit more caution than a bare few seconds allow. Second, travel from a body's surface to beyond the 0.1 G range typically requires at least several minutes, varying with the size of the body.

Exact times are left to the GM as a plot element; the following list suggests typical samples. Note that these sample times are cumulative: that is, a trip from the surface of the Earth to the surface of the moon would add the time from Earth's surface to orbit, from orbit to 0.1 G, from Earth to Moon, from 0.1 G to lunar orbit, and from lunar orbit to the surface.

Time from Surface to Orbit and Vice Versa: Roughly 1-10 minutes, depending upon planetary size, atmospheric conditions, and vessel thrust.

Time from Orbit to 0.1 G and Vice Versa: Roughly 10-30 minutes, depending upon planetary size, vessel thrust, and amount of traffic. Some very small bodies may require considerably less (or none).

Time from Planet to Its Moons and Vice Versa: Mere seconds from the planet's 0.1 G point to a moon's 0.1 G point, under Isler Drive. Hours to days under normal fusion drive.

Time from Planet to Planet (Same System): Mere minutes (inner planets) to several hours (outer planets) under Isler Drive. Hours to days, or longer, for normal fusion drive.

Standard Ships

"I don't care if we do have a luxury model—I just don't like hauling a meatwagon. It's spooky with all those frozen people just a few feet away."

—P.F.C. Vladimir Lanovich

Veteran synths know standard ship configurations and, as mentioned above, have a jargon referring to many of the components. Officially, a ship is known by a code referring to its components. A combat lander would be a B3-S5-C3-T13-D3J66-O12. This means it has the following modules: Bridge 3, Sleeper 5, Crew 3, Transport 1 and 3, Drive 3 with six Drive J units on top and another six underneath, and Options 1 and 2. Some synths would called this a "luxury liner with a basket and toybox."

The following box lists a number of standard ship configurations, some of which are illustrated on the following pages:

Standard Ship Configurations

Combat Lander (lands and supports a small force): B3-S5-C3-T13-D3J66-O12

Rescue Lander[1] (rescues and retrieves civilians): B2-S3-C2-T123-D3J66-O13

Space Battleship (fights other starships): B3-S2-C2-T1-D2J44-O123

System Cruiser (guards a settled system): B1-S2-C2-T1-D2J2

Explorer (explores and surveys new systems): B2-S2-C3-T1-D3J6

Colonizer (takes civilians to settle a planet): B2-S2-C2-T1123-D3J6

Heavy Cargo Hauler (transports large loads): B1-S1-C1-T113-D3J6

Scout[2] (scouts and reports to planet or large ship): B1-D1

Fighter[3] (supports combat operations): B3-D1J2-O123

Local Courier (short distance messenger): B1-S1-D1

Interstellar Courier (long distance messenger): B1-S1-D1J2

Light Cargo Hauler (transports small loads): B1-T1-D2J2

---

1. Completely empty, a standard rescue lander weighs 575 tons, so will exceed Jump 20 with Drive 3J66. Therefore, regulations require a rescue lander with Drive 3J66 to carry at least 25 tons of cargo, bringing its speed down to Jump 20.
2. With an upgrade to Drive 1J22, a scout can attain approximately Jump 41. Though against regulations, this modified small ship (known by synths as a dangermouse) is sometimes used to quickly deliver emergency messages.
3. Because a fighter is so small, its Option package (one Anti-Craft Battery, one chaff launcher, and a few maneuvering thrusters) totals only 10 tons.

Chapter 6: Ships

Starship Modules Compartment Layouts

1 square = 2 feet

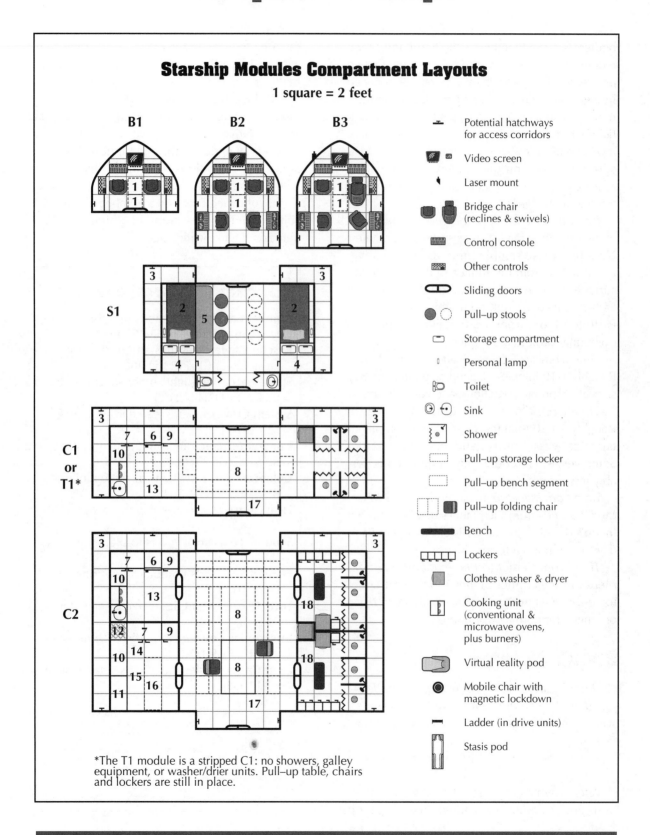

B1 **B2** **B3**

S1

C1 or T1*

C2

Potential hatchways for access corridors

Video screen

Laser mount

Bridge chair (reclines & swivels)

Control console

Other controls

Sliding doors

Pull–up stools

Storage compartment

Personal lamp

Toilet

Sink

Shower

Pull–up storage locker

Pull–up bench segment

Pull–up folding chair

Bench

Lockers

Clothes washer & dryer

Cooking unit (conventional & microwave ovens, plus burners)

Virtual reality pod

Mobile chair with magnetic lockdown

Ladder (in drive units)

Stasis pod

*The T1 module is a stripped C1: no showers, galley equipment, or washer/drier units. Pull–up table, chairs and lockers are still in place.

Chapter 6: Ships

1. Trapdoor to airlock
2. Sleep compartment
3. Access corridor
4. Storage locker
5. Pull–out table
6. Refrigerator
7. Cupboard with shelves
8. Pull–up table
9. Closet
10. Counter
11. Laboratory equipment console
12. Power nexus
13. Galley
14. Sickbay
15. Laboratory
16. Pull–up convalescent bed
17. Mess/meeting room
18. Locker room
19. Locking cell with bunk
20. Locking brig exercise room or holding cell
21. Brig guard post
22. Audio–visual console
23. Gym with workout machines & aerobics mat
24. Ice loader
25. Fusion drive
26. Airlock
27. Rotating and lifting platform
28. Descending ramp, opens down for aft exit

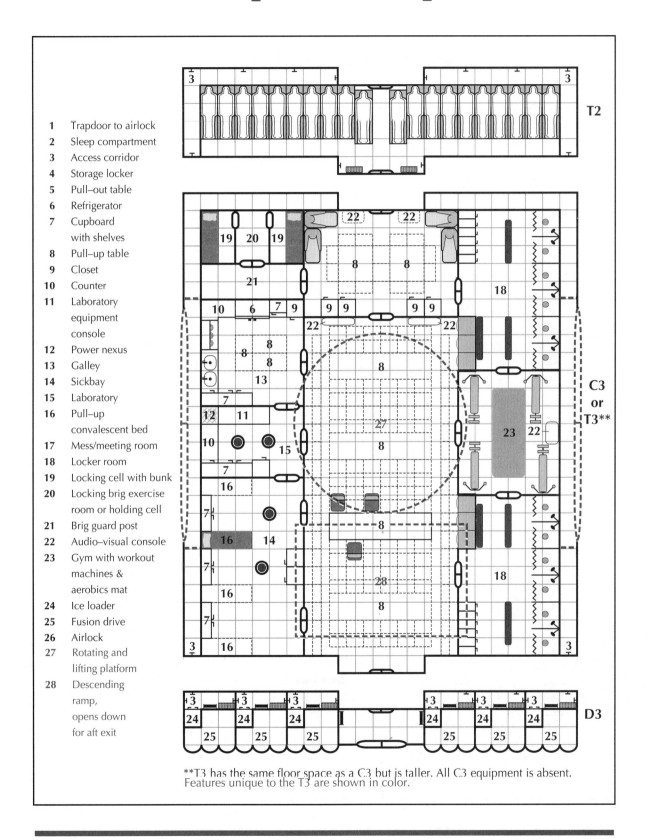

T2

C3 or T3**

D3

**T3 has the same floor space as a C3 but is taller. All C3 equipment is absent. Features unique to the T3 are shown in color.

Chapter 6: Ships

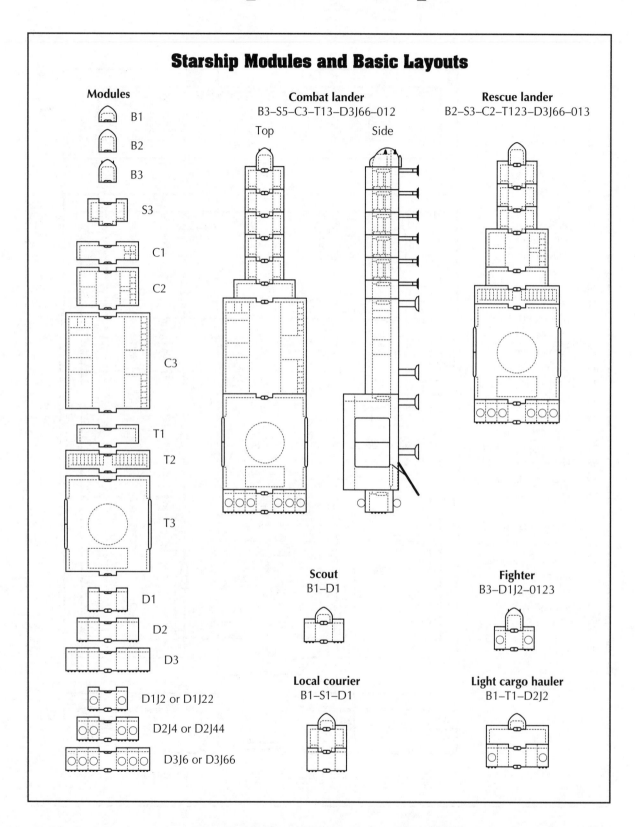

Starship Modules and Basic Layouts

Modules

B1

B2

B3

S3

C1

C2

C3

T1

T2

T3

D1

D2

D3

D1J2 or D1J22

D2J4 or D2J44

D3J6 or D3J66

Combat lander
B3–S5–C3–T13–D3J66–012

Top

Side

Rescue lander
B2–S3–C2–T123–D3J66–013

Scout
B1–D1

Fighter
B3–D1J2–0123

Local courier
B1–S1–D1

Light cargo hauler
B1–T1–D2J2

Chapter 7: L-5 (Stargate)

Seen from space, Stargate—the permanent space station positioned at L-5—resembles a giant four-spoked wheel hovering above the Earth. Exactly 10 kilometers in diameter, its outer rim is sheathed in space rock to protect against asteroids and other debris. UTRPF has devoted several gunships for bigger, more dangerous rocks, as well as pirates, terrorists, or hostile aliens. Also on the rim are the station's dark solar panels which gather light and other energy for the use of those who live within. Stargate has an artificial gravity comparable with Terra's due to the wheel's rotation.

Ships dock in the center of the wheel where the spokes meet. Here, in the zero-gravity of the Hub, the ships are loaded and unloaded. Ferried to one of the four elevators on the Hub's sides, both cargo and passengers eventually head down one of the spokes toward the outer rim.

The Ryan Shield

The entirety of Stargate is protected by the Ryan Shield, an electrical construct designed to deflect harmful space radiation and particles from the station. The generator is located in the Hub and spreads its field around the entire station. It is effective only against subatomic particles and wave energy; larger debris can pass through the field with little problem (Stargate has other defenses for those; see below). Secondary Ryan Shield generators located along the rim can power up and kick in within a minute should the main generator fail for any reason.

The Composition of Stargate

The shell of rock on the outer rim extends approximately 70 meters. Immediately under this is a layer of foam sealant 30 meters thick, designed to protect against the possibility of larger space particles penetrating into the habitable section of Stargate and to seal the hole as quickly as possible if the unthinkable occurs.

Spread through the sealant is an alarm sensor net which alerts technicians when breach has occurred. The sealant is effective for holes as large as 10 meters in diameter and will hold the hole shut for five hours. In case the alarms fail to alert the administration, there are automatic airlocks set in bulkheads around the station. A sudden drop in atmospheric pressure in one area will cause the doors to swing shut, preventing further air loss from the rest of Stargate. Unfortunately, this leaves the inhabitants of that section to fend for themselves until the hole can be mended. For this reason, most individual buildings are fitted with airlocks which activate automatically in an emergency.

Above the sealant runs the subway. The train traverses the entire station, making frequent stops for passengers. Whenever the subway passes into a different Zone, passengers unlicensed for travel in that Zone must debark and wait for the Express to come to the station. The Express stops only at the Embarkation/Debarkation points in each Zone, making a complete loop of Stargate every 20 minutes.

The subway stations also allow access into the ductwork of Stargate. Only licensed technicians have permission to travel the air ducts, and there are 3 guards posted at each station to deal with trouble and to ensure that no one with ulterior motives slips in. The service access tunnels run alongside and above the subway, branching out through Stargate. They are tall enough for a 180 cm human, though they are only comfortable for one who is either incredibly flexible or unnaturally skinny. The humid, cramped tunnels are not even protected by airlocks, except where they abut the subway and accesses.

50 meters above the subways is the "ground level." This is where the main populace of Stargate lives, works, and plays. The variety is typical of any city containing 100,000 people, though there are more rules imposed on what can and cannot be sold than on Terran cities.

An interesting feature of the outer walls and ceiling along the edge of Stargate's residential

Chapter 7: L-5 (Stargate)

zone are the viewscreens installed there. Though they are not actual windows, their images are supplied by cameras mounted on the outer rim and they provide the current visuals of the starfield outside Stargate. Though this can prove disorienting to those who have never seen it before, the general populace of Stargate takes it for granted.

The air above ground level extends 70 meters before it encounters the atmosphere containers, sheeting, and solar panels. Viewscreens placed here show the Hub of the wheel and the stars beyond. If they wish, citizens can watch ships dock and take off or witness space-suited personnel go about their duties in zero-G. The sealant layer is about 20 meters thick here, secreted under a 10-meter wall of titanium, which in turn is hidden behind 10 meters of ceramic shielding.

Living in Stargate

The horizon of Stargate is exactly opposite that of Terra and can be extremely disorienting. The floor curves *up* instead of down, and the horizon is caused by the ceiling rather than the floor or ground. Fortunately for those who might let this affect them, the frequent bulkheads and airlocks prevent exposure of too much of this curvature.

There is neither day nor night on Stargate. There are therefore three artificially imposed cycles to regulate the schedules of citizens. Each cycle is exactly 8 hours long, making a 24-hour day, of which there are seven a week. The days are measured in military time (e.g., 8 am is 0800 hours while 8 pm is 2000 hours) but are otherwise undifferentiated.

Because there is a constant demand for business, nothing on Stargate ever closes. Whether you're looking for a bar, a restaurant, a casino, or a shop, any establishment you find will be open.

What follows is a description of the five Zones that comprise Stargate. The subheading labelled "Access" at the beginning of each section indicates who may enter that area and how freely they can move about while there. The numbers in the descriptions below are keyed to the maps on page 83. The letters at the bottom and top of each close-up map conform to their position on the circular map of Stargate.

A-B. Civilian Area
Access: Anyone can travel through the Civilian Area, and it is here that the bulk of Stargate's human population can be found.

1. Businesses: This is the money hub of Stargate, located conveniently close to the Administration Area (**24**). Nearly all the businesses on Stargate—be they concerned with money, entertainment, or power—have at least some representation in this section.

If the player characters are allowed away from the UTRPF Base, they can find any legitimate service they might want in this section, though the price might be more than they can afford. Banks, shops, and offices offering services of all kinds flourish here.

2. Housing: The housing here is mostly for technicians, factory laborers, office workers, shopkeepers, and their families. It divides into slightly drab and dingy areas for the lower-income earners and stylish ones for their more wealthy counterparts. Most of the homes are rental units in housing complexes 10-stories or more in height with four 3-bedroom apartments per floor.

There are a few small parks here for the use of the populace which help lessen the feeling of being closed in. They are very popular and always have some visitors.

Occasionally, street gangs pop up to "protect" their territory. They are tolerated until they start indulging in criminal activity or begin harassing honest citizens.

3. Colonists: The Colonists' area is a featureless environment of row after row of houses. The mess hall located near the elevator shaft dishes out relatively tasteless institutional food. Every aspect of this area suggests that it is a temporary home, one that has been used countless times by

Chapter 7: L-5 (Stargate)

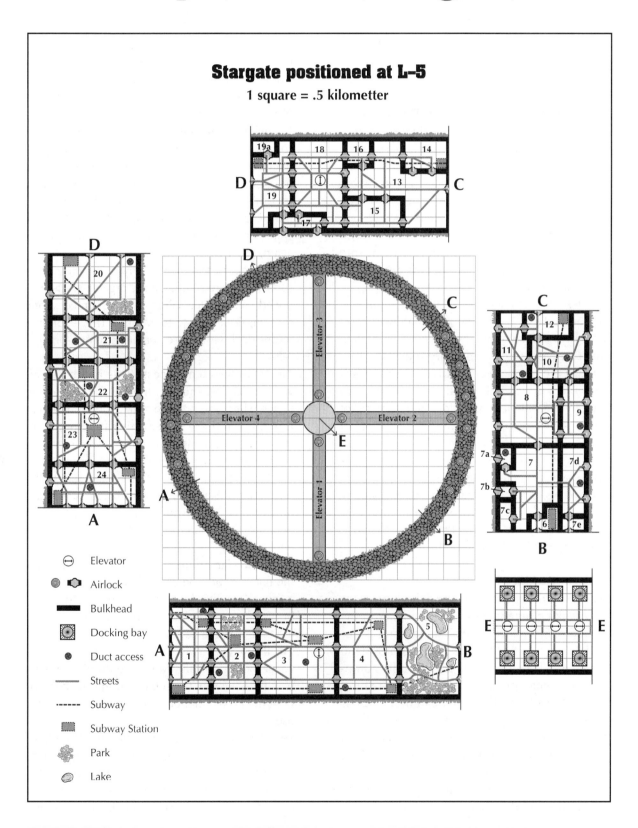

Stargate positioned at L-5

1 square = .5 kilometter

Elevator 3

Elevator 4

Elevator 2

Elevator 1

Legend:

⊖ Elevator

◉ 🔲 Airlock

▬ Bulkhead

▦ Docking bay

◉ Duct access

— Streets

--- Subway

▨ Subway Station

❀ Park

⬭ Lake

countless families and endured through it all. Most colonists are glad to leave this place behind them, no matter how inhospitable the world to which they travel.

4. Entertainment/Black Market: This area contains music, theaters, 3-D entertainment, restaurants, casinos, and a thriving black market. The easily located entertainment is as exciting as one could ask for this side of New Orleans and about as affordable. The black market can provide nearly any illegal service one could ask, but for a price far beyond what it would cost on Terra. Since it is quite difficult to smuggle items into Stargate, affording these services is difficult for the "monetarily challenged." Many, however, find the service rendered well worth the price.

5. Resort Area: The fabulously wealthy of Terra are always looking for new and exotic places to visit. One of Stargate's primary sources of revenue is the resort area, which, for an astonishingly high price, will provide the wealthy with any entertainment they desire amid a setting of trees, lakes, lodge houses, and the vastness of space. The viewscreens normally found spaced about every 10 meters apart elsewhere in Stargate cover the entire wall of the resort area, giving tourists the feeling that outer space is simply a sheet of plastic away, instead of about 100 meters. Everything else in the resort is authentic; nothing less than the best for these folk.

B-C. The Facilities

Access: Only the technicians who work here and ranking bureaucrats can disembark in the Facilities. Since the Facilities are responsible for maintaining life on Stargate, UTRPF guards stand watch at all stations to ensure that only authorized folk enter this area. The Facilities are most notable for the fact that one can hardly cross more than 10 meters before having to duck, twist, or otherwise avoid some of the pipes that go everywhere. None are allowed into this Zone without a vacuum suit.

6. Preliminary Airlock: This airlock allows workers to disembark and suit up before entering their respective areas. Also, given the sheer volume of external airlocks located in the Facilities Zone, this area acts as a kind of insurance to keep blow-outs in this Zone from affecting the rest of the Station.

7. Reclamatories/Recycling: This area is an environmentalist's dream. Every bit of waste produced by the inhabitants of the station is returned here, where it is broken down for fertilizer, recombined, or refined into another product. Nothing on Stargate is wasted, whether air, water, or solids; everything finds its way into use again, one way or another.

The main room, dotted by huge vats, is responsible for recycling all the organic waste produced on Stargate. Solid waste is shunted to one section, liquid waste to another. The secondary rooms deal with the reclamation of non-organic refuse.

7a. Main Service Access: This hatch allows workers to descend into the bowels of Stargate to see where the problems may lurk. Since malfunctions in these systems threaten the life of everyone on Stargate, technicians are constantly watching for any problems that may arise.

7b. Main Hatch: The most prominent exit to the inner ring of Stargate, the Hatch sees a constant flow of traffic of personnel in vacuum suits. From here they spread across the station, to deal with whatever task they have been assigned.

7c. Air Reclamation: This room filters the air for the entire station. In case of breakdown, there is a secondary filter located in the main room of **7**, but it has had to kick into use only once in all the time Stargate has been in service.

7d. Refineries: Any non-organic product discarded by the inhabitants eventually finds its way here, where it is separated into its component materials, melted down, and reformed for use again.

7e. Control Room: The "trouble board" for Stargate is here, the nerve nexus of the entire station. All of the alarms located throughout the depths of the station are wired into this room, so that trained professionals can immediately pinpoint a

Chapter 7: L-5 (Stargate)

problem and deal with it before it spreads. All the walls of this area are covered with information panels—blinking lights, detailed maps of sections of Stargate, and a vast array of buttons controlling most of the station's systems.

8. Cargo Bay: This heavily-guarded area is the repository for all material that comes from or goes to the ships docking at the Hub. Whether it is food and supplies for colonists or heavy ore from one of the mining outposts, this is where it is temporarily warehoused while awaiting inspection and loading.

9. Factories: Almost all the non-organic goods manufactured on Stargate are made in this foul-smelling and gringy (but highly efficient) area. By-products and industrial wastes are returned to area **7** for recycling.

10. Food/Water: Responsible for producing food for the entirety of Stargate (excluding the resort, which has fresh delicacies flown in daily from Earth), the technicians here get most of their raw material from area **7**. Although most of the food produced here has the tired taste of reconstituted rations, it is highly nourishing. Food is also freeze-packed and dehydrated here for long-term storage.

11. Laboratories: These are secondary research facilities for the scientists engaged in area **21**. They are required to use this area for their more dangerous experiments, as it is shielded from the rest of the station. This entire area is kept antiseptically clean.

12. Garage: This is the garage for the heavy moving equipment used both outside and inside the Facilities. All vehicles must be checked out at the beginning of each shift and returned at the end of the same shift.

C-D. UTRPF Zone

Access: Only the military, or those with an authorized military escort, can travel through the UTRPF Zone. The few exceptions involve high officials of United Terra. Five synners guard each station to ensure that this rule is strictly enforced.

13. Training Area: A region this big is ideal for training exercises involving endurance and stealth. Though the training weapons and vehicles cause no damage to their targets, they make for a serious scare. This is the area for general warfare training; there are more specialized zones further along the ring.

14. PX: The general store/bar/mess hall of the UTRPF Zone, the PX is a favorite hangout of off-duty synners. Nowhere else can they expect to find relaxation and general acceptance for their synthetic nature. They can also get drinks, buy extra food, and perhaps find some lucky charm for their next mission.

15. The Rookery: These barracks are the homes of newly created synners, who are kept in different dormitories from their more-experienced brethern until their training is complete. These dormitories, like the colonists' homes in area **3**, are only temporary quarters completely lacking in character.

16. Training Area: Though only about one kilometer square, this is the most intense training grounds UTRPF could devise. The terrain and climate in this room can be shifted to simulate conditions on other planets. Unfortunately, it is almost never as brutal as the real thing.

17. Vacuum Training Prep Area: Numerous vacuum suits and mock weapons are stored here. UTRPF recruits suit up here before they exit onto the ring of Stargate to practice combat in low-G.

18. Barracks: This large area is home to the experienced synners and a favorite hangout for off-duty UTRPFers. The buildings are divided by daytime duty cycle; those on the first cycle (from 0000 to 0800 hours) sleep in different barracks than those on cycle 2 (0800 to 1600 hours) or cycle 3 (1600 to 2400 hours). Each barrack has its own character and a tradition of friendly rivalry between different barracks exists.

19. Military Administration: The administration area is designed to keep a close watch over the synners stationed on Stargate. It is situated between the human and synthetic personnel to minimize contact between the two; the only humans synners see on a regular basis are their immediate superiors. The area is functional and clean; like everything in the military, it has no more frills than necessary. The stockade is located here, as well as the offices of the human commanding officers.

19a. Armory: All heavy-duty weaponry and ammunition is kept in this area adjoining the Administration area. They are kept securely guarded by human personnel to keep the synners from staging an effective mutiny. Weapons must be checked out of here before a mission, and they will only be released to those authorized to use them. Synners trying to obtain weapons illegally are tranquilized and sent to the stockade for court-martial.

D-A. Administration/Research

Access: Theoretically, anyone can travel through the Administration/Research Zone. However, no one is allowed to enter a building without a special permit or *very* good reason. Only in the Stargate Administration area (**24**) are citizens really free to come and go as they wish.

20. Human Military Housing: Here is where UTRPF's human officers live when off-duty; it is, naturally, a nicer area in which to live than the barracks afforded to the synners. This area has all the amenities given to the synths (PX, mess hall, etc.). If the personnel here desire to train alongside the synners, they can travel to the various training grounds in the other areas.

21. Research and Development: Both UTRPF and private companies pursue various types of research here, ranging from weapon development to aerosols. Each laboratory has a compound that covers at least 10,000 square meters and its own hired guards to keep the inquisitive outside.

22. Admin/Research Housing: Though their assistants live in area **2**, the top-flight scientists and the highest-ranking bureaucrats of Stargate make their homes in this posh area. Though the apartments are still stacked in buildings of 10 stories, there is but one apartment per floor. The ordinary folk of Stargate are discouraged from coming to this area to prevent them from growing jealous of those who enjoy such luxury.

23. Colonial Offices: This area, located conveniently near the elevator, is home to the colonial offices of United Terra. Any colonists with questions, requests, or problems may come to this area seeking assistance. The offices here are also responsible for coordinating reports from the various colonies, administrating and allocating colonists, and planning further expeditions. They have worked very closely with UTRPF since the trouble with the "bugs" began.

24. Stargate Administration: This is, in effect, the City Hall of Stargate. Officials here deal with the problems of the residents, plan further additions and improvements to the station, administer the Public Works, and oversee the daily running of the station. There is a trouble-board here identical to that found in the Facilities (area **7e**).

E. Launching Area (Hub)

Access: Everyone on Stargate travels through the Launching Area at some time or another; the number of people who constantly return is far smaller. Only technicians trained to dock ships and unload cargo can come and go through the Hub without question. Because of the scientific experiments being conducted here, scientists with legitimate reasons for being in the Hub are also allowed through security upon presentation of proper credentials.

Besides being the landing/launching/refueling/refitting area, some research is also conducted in labs located in those areas of the Hub furthest from the docking facilities. It is, scientists claim, an ideal area in which to study the effects of zero-G. With the blessing of UT, they have a sizeable area in which to run their experiments.

Chapter 8:
Running the BUGHUNTERS™ Game

Just as players must be able to relate to the role of UTRPF troopers in order to play them effectively, GMs must be able to relate to the game world if they are to run it effectively. It is the purpose of this chapter, then, to familiarize you with the secrets lurking behind the scenes of the BUGHUNTERS™ milieu. Along the way, we'll discuss some tricks of the GM's trade and give guidelines for such things as awarding experience points.

Note that while plot elements are covered in this chapter, the basics of designing adventures and running NPCs are covered in their respective chapters, rather than here.

A Friendly Warning: Players should read no further in this book. Learning the secrets here and in the following chapters prematurely will only rob you of the fun of discovering them during play. If you *must* read them, at least be a serious enough role-player to pretend you do not know them while playing your character.

Central Premise

> *"Life and death are fatally interbred. The verdant grass grows; the rapacious deer rips it up and eats. The delicate deer grows; the blood-thirsty cougar rips it up and eats. The worm feeds the fish which feeds the person who, ultimately, feeds the worm. And even the pacifist vegetarian murders the lettuce."*
>
> —J. R. Reyes, 21st-century philosopher

Despite its beauty, Nature can be savage at times. But even in its most predacious moments, life on Terra could not begin to prepare humanity's first stellar explorers psychologically for the sheer, inimical hostility of space and the worlds around other stars. In journeying to the stars, humans are learning that colonizing alien planets involves much more than simply coming to terms with rugged new environments: there are *things* lurking out there, murderously hateful creatures that delight in slaughter and that kill in the most hideous, senselessly cruel ways.

What humans don't understand is *why* extra-solar space is proving to be so unnaturally hostile. But it's something that you, as GM, need to know in order to run a BUGHUNTERS campaign.

The "backdrop" premise of the BUGHUNTERS game is that there has been for untold ages a bitter battle being fought among the stars—the Ancients' War. The two primary alien races involved (collectively called the Ancients) have, from time to time, conscripted other, minor races into the fight, most of whom are now, as a result, extinct. After millennia of strife, the Ancients have battled their way to a virtual stalemate. Now the few remaining Ancients of either race are holed up in a handful of highly secret, heavily protected outposts, venturing forth only to seed contested planets with nightmarish creations of their alien sciences, in order to deny use of those planets to their enemy, and to launch guerilla attacks against any target that presents itself.

It is into this battleground that humanity, all unsuspecting, is stepping in its bid for the stars—a devastated warzone in which anything that moves is considered a fair target.

Theme, Mood, and Pacing

Thematically, BUGHUNTERS adventures revolve around two main elements: action and horror. On the one hand, PCs are larger-than-life heroes carrying heavy weaponry who get to voyage among the stars. On the other, they end up facing horribly vicious creatures that are part of a threat so extensive as to remain virtually a perpetual mystery to them. Their first priority should be to stablize a rapidly deteriorating situation by rescuing colonists from murderous aliens and protecting worlds from further attacks. Only after this difficult task is accomplished can continued exploration and expansion safely resume. Fortunately, they are able to make real gains against the threat to humanity, not just through military

Chapter 8:
Running the BUGHUNTERS™ Game

action but also by advancing human knowledge of the situation.

Of course, maintaining those themes requires some finesse upon the GM's part. Without that expertise, a BUGHUNTERS™ campaign can devolve into little more than an endless string of combats. And while combat is a central element of the game, without the inclusion of storytelling elements you might just as well be playing a boardgame. But with a bit of care, you can guide your campaign to become a gripping drama of fascinating characters battling frightening odds, and overcoming them. The raw material is there, in the player characters and their individual histories. It merely requires the right atmosphere to let it bloom. Let's consider some specific topics involved in maintaining that atmosphere.

Pacing

Remember that we earlier characterized BUGHUNTERS campaigns as a blend of action and horror. Maintaining a truly effective action theme is primarily a matter of pacing. We've all heard in high school literature classes that a plot has rising action, leading to a climax, and then a bit of winding down (denoument). That's not a bad model to work from in our discussion.

Of course, in a novel, the pacing of a plot is firmly in the author's hands. Role-playing games, because they involve several participants rather than one, are not quite so easy to handle. If the GM takes too firm a hand in a plot's development, the players begin to feel they have no choice in things as they are led by the nose from scene to scene. But if the GM simply lets the players proceed at their own pace without any guidance, the game can meander aimlessly, speeding past the most significant story elements and dragging during the dullest ones as the players rush obliviously through important scenes, plod through false starts, and so on.

Pacing is the GM's key to solving this dilemma. With it, GMs can leave their players freedom, yet maintain a satisfactory sense of

drama. What we mean by this is that as GM, you are, in effect, in control of the flow of time. If the PCs are involved in a critically dramatic moment, make it last: give the players dramatic detail and convey the significance of the moment to them by your voice and expression. On the other hand, if the PCs are involved in a relatively insignificant event, you can speed the hands of the clock by keeping description to a minimum.

For example, in BUGHUNTERS adventures there's no need to describe in detail each day of a three-month hyperspace journey, but you definitely should devote detail to the sights, sounds, and smells of a battle. As a guide, ask yourself which of those things would get the most description in a novel. You can apply this question just as well to encounters. Obviously, most novels would not spend as much attention on the clerk who handles the protagonists' launch papers or even on the general who assigned them a mission as on the hospitalized colonist who barely survived an alien attack and is describing it to the heroes.

So let the level of detail and the intensity with which you convey it be your means of controlling drama, without arm-twisting your PCs into a specific line of action.

Mood

The horror of the BUGHUNTERS setting makes the moments of high action even more satisfying and dramatic, giving the PC heroes a heartfelt reason for battling while heightening the fulfillment they feel in defeating their hideous enemies. In other words, the horror in a plot's rising action makes the sense of relief at the climax all the more satisfying.

But horror is a rather tricky emotion to convey, and it becomes an even more difficult proposition when matched with the need for heroism. Let's take a moment to consider why this is so. But in preparation, we must first discuss a related issue of the GM's multiple, sometimes conflicting, roles.

Chapter 8:
Running the BUGHUNTERS™ Game

A GM's Roles: In board games, rules are written to cover a limited set of scenario parameters. Consequently, they can be quite cut-and-dried, and players can look to them as law. Nevertheless, referees are uniformly called for in board game tournament play to serve as dispassionate arbiters of any disputes as to the meaning of those rules.

Historically, role-playing game GMs have often been cast in the same light, as impartial arbiters of the game rules during conflicts of PCs versus enemy NPCs. But a number of problems arise concerning this model.

For one thing, because a role-playing game covers an incredibly wider set of possibilities than does a board game, its rules are, of necessity, more like a framework giving precedents and examples. GMs are called upon not just to interpret rules but to extrapolate from them. This point is especially significant when other differences of approach—such as a GM's job as story director—are considered, because that extrapolation is colored by such things.

For another, it isn't really fair to consider a GM as an impartial arbiter of conflicts between PCs and NPCs. In playing the role of NPCs, the GM becomes one of the *participants* in the conflict, and an arbiter must be, virtually by definition, a disinterested *third* party.

This is further complicated by the fact that in creating adventures for the PCs to participate in, the GM becomes something of a game designer. Therefore, when the adventure is actually played, the GM may discover that it is less than adequately balanced—that the PCs are either having too easy a time of things (resulting in player boredom) or too difficult a time (resulting in player frustration)—and that some sort of on-the-spot design change is required.

Add to all this a role-playing GM's desire for drama and the necessity to intervene to insure satisfactory pacing, and the image of GM as rules arbiter first and foremost begins to come to pieces. A different model—one of players as actors and GM as director—becomes more use-ful. This is not, of course, to say that the GM should never arbitrate or define rules. Game rules still serve an important function as a framework for play, but as such they are merely servants to the story being experienced.

With these things understood, let's return to the discussion of mood in the BUGHUNTERS™ game. The relation of it all will become apparent as we do so.

The Elements of Horror: Given that horror is an important plot device in BUGHUNTERS adventures, GMs need to understand how to convey it to their players. This can be a bit tricky, but rest assured that the results are well worth the effort.

One element that helps set the stage for fear and horror is isolation. That's why, for instance, starships in the BUGHUNTERS game are relatively small and take months or years to travel from star to star. The PCs (and any attendant NPCs) are entirely on their own during this time, with no way of getting outside help. What's more, even the human outposts they visit are isolated, with small populations, and beleaguered by enormous threats. You should take a few moments to build this tone whenever your PCs travel, describing to them the hollow sound of their ship's halls, the cramped quarters, and the utter silence between the stars. Even on Earth the PCs are effectively isolated by the mistrust, fear, and anger normal humans demonstrate toward them as clones.

Another important element of horror is a sense of mystery. This is why most adventures will require the PCs to figure out what their opponent is before they can even begin to seriously battle it. By the same token, when you run their foes, have the creatures lurk in shadow, springing out and attacking the PCs unexpectedly. Monsters in the BUGHUNTERS universe tend to have high Psyche and Reflexes attributes, giving them a good chance of surprising the PCs and allowing them to close very quickly in combat. Don't let the PCs have time to fully register a monster's appearance; rather, give the

Chapter 8:
Running the BUGHUNTERS™ Game

players a rushed description of the most dangerous-looking features, focusing on dramatic effect ("It's roughly human-sized, black and shiny-wet, with spiky shoulders, wicked claws, and a mouthful of glistening fangs at least 20 cm long, and it's running right at you!"). If you describe creatures in too much detail, they have a tendency to become mundane and lose their horrific mystique.

Note that this once again returns us to the issue of pacing. You must choose when to give long, moody descriptions and when to switch to short, rushed, hectic glimpses. Through a judicious blend of suspense and crises, you can keep players alert and apprehensive, continually on edge about what will happen next.

Of course, players who care about their characters will feel a certain amount of anxiety whenever those characters are in a dangerous situation. Dramatic GMs have an edge on this issue, because they convey atmosphere in such a way as to make their players feel quite close to

the scene. On the other hand, such GMs tend to avoid killing PCs when possible, under the premises that a) protagonists ought to survive their own stories and b) players grow close to their characters given time but remain distant from them if they die off rapidly. Players in such campaigns may as a result subconsciously come to think of their characters as immune to real peril.

The easiest way to convince such players of their PCs' mortality is to let a PC or two die early in the campaign. And since there's no point in letting a PC die undramatically, your golden rule should be **whenever you have to kill off a PC, do so brutally, for the shock effect**. The first time a situation arises in which the PCs are horribly outclassed and forced to beat a disorganized retreat, one or two of them should be caught and slaughtered while the rest are getting away.

For example, imagine that your PCs are in a swamp, battling a horde of incredibly fast creatures something like meter-tall, carnivorous, reptilian monkeys. Their luck with combat rolls has not been good, and they're almost out of ammunition. You realize that the entire party is in immediate danger of being wiped out, so you decide to have the bugs swarm the nearest one, allowing the other PCs to escape. The unlucky victim's death should be conveyed in a few, carefully chosen details: the bloody muzzles of the "monkeys" as they tear loose chunks of flesh, the gurgling cries of the victim, who is drowning while being torn apart. When the surviving PCs later return with reinforcements and heavier weaponry to slaughter the creatures, the final battle will be all the more dramatic for them because it gives them a chance to avenge their friend. Once you've proved your willingness to kill PCs, your players won't casually assume that their PCs are safe in your hands and will work harder to have their PCs survive.

Another important element of horror is a sense of permanent loss. Killing NPCs that the PCs have grown close to and come to depend on is an excellent way of invoking this sense of loss,

Chapter 8:
Running the BUGHUNTERS™ Game

and thereby giving the PCs a solid reason for battling the alien invaders. Similarly, taking away part of the PCs' "roots" by having them see their donors killed in a nasty incursion of bugs on Earth or the PCs' homes on Stargate wrecked by a runaway bug adds the very powerful motive of revenge to a BUGHUNTERS™ campaign, giving the characters a personal stake in the war.

Killing NPCs can be useful in another way as well. You can use it as a sort of "countdown to doom" for the PCs. That is, you can surround the PCs with NPCs, then have the bugs kill off those NPCs one by one. Soon "ten little Indians" paranoia should set in: as the body count rises, the pool of potential victims becomes ever smaller. Suspense will mount among the players as death creeps ever closer to their characters. Even in all-out combats, NPCs should be the first to fall as a general rule. From the standpoint of creating fiction, targeting the minor characters (NPCs) first is a legitimate tactic, thereby establishing the deadliness of the adventure milieu while saving the main characters (the PCs) for the climax. Even if your players realize that you are giving their characters preferential treatment, the tactic works nicely, particularly if you time things well. That is, if the players realize that they are only halfway through the adventure and already all but one or two of the NPCs are dead, they will definitely begin to worry.

Once again, pacing becomes important. For an NPC's death to upset the players, the PCs must have come to care about that person. That means the GM has to have taken the time to role-play that character in such a way that the PCs will genuinely miss having the NPC around. For relatively helpless NPCs such as children, the time will be less, because care for them is sort of "hardwired" into us as humans; adult NPCs will take a bit more work. Remember, too, that an element of horror is surprise. Players will quickly come to recognize bugfodder and refuse to invest any emotion in an NPC who was obviously created just to be killed off. As a GM, don't rely on one particular trick too often; keep your players off-balance.

You should be aware, however, that too much horror can sometimes be worse than not enough. Humans aren't constructed to maintain intense emotions for long periods of time. Eventually, they become jaded to even the worst horrors if they are piled on too thick (Shakespeare's *Titus Andronicus* serves as a good demonstration of this, at least for modern audiences). If NPCs are dropping like flies and monsters are jumping at the PCs from every dark corner, your players may overload and begin treating the adventure as slapstick comedy. Suspense requires highs and lows, so remember to interweave scenes of relative quiet to throw the shocks into relief.

Finally, keep firmly in mind that the purpose of the horror in BUGHUNTERS adventures is largely to heighten the sense of heroism when the horrific is overcome. Again, this requires a deft touch on the GM's part: too much horror and the players feel overwhelmed, more victimized than heroic; too little horror, and adventures become colorless beast hunts. You should work to pace things so that the PCs are thoroughly horrified for a time, then heroically overcome their enemy.

PC Rewards

After an adventure's climax comes a time in which the PCs reap the rewards of their labors. Those rewards come in a number of different shapes.

Experience

One result of adventuring is, of course, the gaining of experience, represented in the AMAZING ENGINE™ system as experience points. The *System Guide* and page 27 of this book explain how those points may be spent; we explain here how they are to be awarded to PCs in the BUGHUNTERS game. Primarily, experience points represent character growth, mainly through successes but also, to a lesser degree, by failures. Experience points also reward (and thus encourage) good role-playing.

The exact number of experience points to be awarded to an individual is subject to the GM's discretion, as is the appropriate moment for the award. As a general rule, however, it is suggested that awards be given at the end of each session of play, for several reasons: 1) to represent the fact that characters benefit from their attempts even in the midst of trial; 2) to prevent praiseworthy events from being forgotten over the course of a multi-session adventure; and 3) to provide a summary of events for the individual session, giving that session identity as an episode in the ongoing adventure.

In terms of number of points to be awarded per session, GMs can award each player one to five points for each item listed below.

Experience Awards

Level of Threat: The GM should decide just how serious a threat the PC's enemies were this session, on a scale of 1 to 5, and award each PC that number of points. This bonus may be doubled for an adventure's climax.

Level of Success: The group's performance should be judged as a whole, again on a scale of 1 (worst) to 5 (best), and each PC should receive that number of points. This bonus may be doubled for the climactic episode in an adventure.

Quality of Role-playing: Everyone gets 1 point if they at least tried to play their role. Above-average performances gain 2 or 3, and a remarkable performance garners 4 or 5.

PC's Usefulness to the Group: Unreasonably uncooperative characters should receive no points at all, while those who were along for the ride receive a single point. Useful characters should receive 2 or 3 points, and anyone who "saved the day" receives 4 or 5.

Entertainment: Everyone who participated should receive 1 point. Those who did a memorable event should receive 2 or 3. Any-

one who made the whole group break out cheering or laughing should receive 4 or 5. GMs are encouraged to solicit their players' opinions of events in this category.

Note that this award system is rather generous. This is to ensure that PCs have a continual supply of experience points to spend as die roll modifiers during play to improve their chances to survive. GMs can encourage this by occasionally making comments such as, "You really need to make this shot. You might want to spend a few experience points."

Illusory Experience: UTRPF's mental recording equipment enables PCs to experience "virtual reality" training missions. However, make sure that players keep any points earned on such missions separate from their normal total, as these temporary points can only be used to modify die rolls, and that only during the subsequent real mission. At the end of that real mission, any remaining experience points gained from the dry run are lost.

Other Rewards

Experience isn't the only reward for adventures, of course. There are also emotional benefits such as the satisfaction of a job well done, the heartfelt thanks of those who have been aided by the PCs' efforts, military honors, promotion, even extra equipment!

As a GM, you are encouraged to play up the emotional rewards. Take a moment to describe the young parents throwing their arms around the PCs and thanking them profusely for saving their children's lives, the warm salute and handshake they receive from their superior officer during an awards ceremony back at Stargate, the hearty pat on the back and round of drinks from other synners. These can be great moments for you to establish emotional ties with NPCs that you can endanger in later adventures.

As to medals, ribbons, and other such military

Chapter 8:
Running the BUGHUNTERS™ Game

awards, these have no firm game effect—unless as GM you choose to assign them rank point bonuses—but they are wonderful role-playing devices. You should be rather stingy with most of them, especially the higher awards, giving them out only to reflect truly unusual achievement during a mission. With these things in mind, rather than give an exhaustive listing of awards, we provide a list of modern examples to serve as a guideline to the GM's creation of others.

Sample Awards

Letter of Commendation: Given for meritorious service, though of a minor sort. The higher the rank of the officer signing the letter, the more prestigious the award. 1 point per letter.

Purple Heart: Given to anyone wounded in action. Given the dangers synners routinely face, most of them gain this award early in their careers (those that survive, at any rate). 2 points.

Commendation Medal: Given for achievement commended in writing by a Senior Grade officer; always accompanied by a Letter of Commendation. 2 points.

Meritorious Service Medal: Given for outstanding achievement, whether in combat or not. 3 points.

Service Medal: Given for marked valor in combat. 4 points.

Silver Star: Given for meritorious service, greater than that receiving a Meritorious Service Medal. 4 points.

Distinguished Service Medal: Given for even more notably meritorious service. 6 points.

Distinguished Service Cross: Given for outstanding bravery in combat. 8 points.

Medal of Honor: Given for exceptional heroism, usually in battle, but occasionally for non-combat gallantry. 10 points.

As for equipment, your PCs may decide to collect abandoned weapons and the like along the course of an adventure. Remember, however, that the use of those things is subject to your control, as explained in the very next section of this chapter.

Other Issues

Having covered the essentials of running BUGHUNTERS™ adventures, let's tie things up by considering a few more specialized topics.

Adapting to Individual PC Groups

A lot of leeway has been given to the players in terms of what types of characters they may play. Unfortunately, this may mean that you end up with a group of PCs who are missing an important type of personnel.

If the group is long on aerospace PCs, including essential personnel such as pilots, but short on marines, this needn't be a real problem: the aerospace PCs will just have to fill in as ground combat troops. This serves as an excellent rationale for getting them out of the ship when an adventure moves planet-side. You needn't assign any NPCs to the crew if you'd rather not.

On the other hand, if the group is long on marines but short on aerospace personnel, they may be missing essential crewmembers needed for their ship to reach their destination, such as a pilot or engineer. Again, this isn't a terrible problem, as you can assign them NPCs for such positions and create a temporary UTRPF injunction that those persons remain with the ship at all times. As a matter of fact, making such NPCs weak in combat skills gives the PCs yet another thing to worry about: they have to protect them if they ever want to get the ship back to Stargate.

On a different note, remember that what equipment UTRPF assigns for a mission is entirely up to you as GM. Whenever they assign a new mission, they assign equipment for that mission, and you should judge such things based upon how it will affect the unfolding story.

Chapter 8:
Running the BUGHUNTERS™ Game

Besides using this to help balance adventures, you can use it as another way of making the players anxious. That is, if they receive little equipment, they'll worry that they are going to be outclassed; if they receive lots and lots, they'll have to wonder what type of enemy could be so terrible as to require such an outfitting.

Also in your control is the question of how stringently UTRPF inspects what personal equipment the PCs carry on board. UTRPF may perform a surprise inspection of quarters at any time, and they may have objections to synners even possessing certain items, let alone taking them along on official missions.

In deciding such things for each mission, let play balance be your primary guide, but temper your decision with the realization that part of the fun of role-playing is the accumulation of gear, and that players like to have their PCs use what they own, especially if it is unusual. Also, the higher the PCs' rank, and the more successful missions they have completed, the more lenient

UTRPF is likely to be. Nevertheless, even the highest-ranking personnel are subject to military orders. Of course, you can barter with the players a bit, agreeing to let them take a particular item if another is left behind. Or you can declare a size guideline (no unauthorized longarms on a particular mission, for example, although personal pistols might be allowed).

To Fudge, or Not to Fudge

Inevitably during play, the situation will arise where the PCs suddenly find the odds turn overwhelmingly against them because of a few bad rolls. In such cases, there is a temptation for the GM to correct things by "fudging" die rolls—i.e., rolling in secret, then changing the result generated to something more beneficial for the players.

We recommend against this, because once players catch on (and they will) they may begin to feel more like observers than full participants. For the same reason, we recommend against sending along powerful NPCs to shepherd the PCs through difficult adventures; it just isn't fun to watch the GM play both sides of a conflict.

Instead, we recommend that you stretch your imagination to change the odds during a lopsided battle. Sometimes it is as simple as having an enemy switch to attacking a different PC, thus spreading the damage around. At others, it may mean having a new combatant enter the fray—perhaps a previously terrified NPC, a native predator, or even synner reinforcements—to provide a distraction, a pool of new hit points, and a chance for the PCs to regroup and/or get in a couple of extra hits.

If you handle such episodes deftly, your players will never know that you didn't have things planned that way from the start, and you'll have solved the problem without fudging a single roll. Take a little extra time when designing an adventure to include a back-up plan for each potentially disastrous combat; it's a much more satisfying way of changing the odds for everyone concerned.

Chapter 9: Nonplayer Characters

A glance through this chapter will readily reveal that the title is somewhat misleading, that most of the creatures included are aliens of one sort or another, and that not all of them can properly be called "characters." There is a good reason for this deception: it is to help maintain in players initially a fiction of normalcy in the universe. Allow us to explain.

Because the game is set at the very beginning of humanity's exploration of the stars, the race has no idea of the threats that it is soon to face. Players should think of their characters as approaching a vast unknown. Initially, the PCs are sent to find out why contact is being lost with Earth's colonies and outpost worlds. All they know is that there's *something* out there, and that whatever it is has wiped out three of humanity's six colonies outside the Solar System in the last seven years. It is only over the course of time that they begin to piece together exactly what is happening, and why.

With this in mind, the title "Nonplayer Characters" seems much more innocuous than "Aliens and Monsters," for example. It is a subtle point, but a valid one, and it helps protect for the GM a sense of mystery among the players.

NPC Motivations

A significant part of GMing any role-playing game involves convincingly playing the roles of all the NPCs your players' characters will meet in the course of their adventures. How you play those NPCs will largely determine how your players play their own characters. Sketchy NPCs that are little more than props will lead your players to treat the adventure campaign lightly. But if your NPCs seem like real people, with motivations and histories of their own, your players will respond in kind, identifying strongly with their own characters and buying into the fictive universe you jointly create.

Playing convincing NPCs is actually not that difficult a task. Primarily, it is a matter of reacting to the PCs from an understanding of each NPC's personal motivations—not necessarily your motivations as GM. That is, as GM, you may plan to use a particular NPC—let's say a panicked penal colonist named Dwight—to give the PCs a bit of foreknowledge about a deadly alien creature that is headed their way. Your GM motivation is to give them information. Dwight, however, has a much more immediate motivation: he wants to get in the PCs' ship, to get into the air and away from the creature . . . desperately. His personal motivation won't prompt him to blithely stand around and chat with the PCs long enough to give them a description of the creature in detail. Rather, he wants to convince them to take him and leave—now! But fortunately, his motivation can serve yours, and in a manner more likely to excite your players. As GM, you prepare for the scene by taking a moment (say a breath or two) to settle mentally and emotionally into the personality of Dwight, and then you launch into the encounter. It might go something like this:

Dwight, running toward the PCs, gasping: "We've got to get into the ship! Hurry!"

A PC: "Wait a minute. Just settle down. What's the problem?"

Dwight: "There's something coming! We've got to get away, now!"

A PC: "No one's going anywhere until you settle down and tell us what's up. Understand? Now, what's got you so excited?"

Dwight: "This . . . *thing* . . . it busted right through the cement wall! It grabbed Jackson and tore him right in two. I hit it with a chair—a metal one—but it just bounced off; it's got some kind of armor shell. One of the guards hit it with a shotgun blast, but all that did was get its attention: it jumped ten meters, easy, landed right on him, and knocked his head clean off. Come on! It'll be here any minute! Let's go!"

Notice that despite Dwight's panic, quite a bit of important information is conveyed to the PCs in this exchange: the creature is incredibly strong; it is armored; it is quick and can jump;

Chapter 9:
Nonplayer Characters

it is roughly human-sized (implied by the general description); it is murderously vicious. But what's more, some of Dwight's alarm will certainly be transmitted to the PCs as well, increasing the players' excitement for the coming encounter with the creature.

As you read through the NPC descriptions in this chapter, you'll see that the bulk of each is an overview of the NPC's motivations and behavior; this will help you easily assume the NPC's persona and bring that character or creature to life, so to speak. Stats are important, of course, but they are only the skeleton of an NPC. It is motivation and behavior that give a character flesh and blood, and that make role-playing something more than board-gaming.

NPC Skills

Rather than insist that the GM adhere slavishly to a particular list of skills for each of the NPC types described in this chapter, we leave it to you to decide during play, as need for a particular skill arises, whether or not the NPC in question has that skill.

Creating New NPCs

As your BUGHUNTERS™ campaign progresses, you will almost certainly need to go beyond the characters and creatures listed in this chapter to design new ones of your own.

Designing human or synner NPCs is not a very difficult proposition: simply use the PC design sequence and the human NPCs listed in this chapter as a guide, adjusting them as you see fit.

Designing alien creatures is nearly as simple a task. Again, you may use the creatures in this chapter as guides, then adjust their stats and abilities to your needs. Note that any technology you give to alien races may greatly affect the tone of your campaign. If your PCs regularly face sentient mechanical cities, aliens with weapons of super-science, and the like, the campaign will

have a very different feel from one in which they generally face voracious creatures of animal intelligence. In the descriptions that follow, we give you a mix of the spectrum of possibilities for you to choose among them for the particular tone you desire.

NPC Categories

For ease of reference, nonplayer characters in this game can be divided into three basic categories: the Ancients, Xenoforms, and Terrans.

The Ancients

Those portions of the galaxy in humanity's immediate vicinity have been largely devastated by an on-going, ages-old conflict between two primary sapient alien races, each now nearly exhausted from century upon century of battle. At one time or another, several other minor sapient races have been conscripted into the war on one side or the other; most of them are now extinct as a result, while others have some few fugitive survivors. The Ancients is the collective term by which these minor races came to speak of the two principal combatants. When speaking of the Ancient races individually, they came to use the terms Shapers and Artificers.

Please note that encounters with these prime movers of the conflict should be extremely rare, coming only at the dramatic culmination of an entire campaign. The Ancients are, themselves, nearly extinct. Their remnants dwell on small hidden bases scattered throughout the galaxy, from which they stir only occasionally, when directly threatened or when an opportunity presents itself to strike a telling blow against their enemies. Consequently, they operate primarily as powers behind the scenes, the ones who set the stage long ago and who still occasionally meddle with other races, typically by proxy, through agents (biological or technological) designed specifically for that purpose. Nevertheless, we describe them here in some detail so

Chapter 9:
Nonplayer Characters

that you may more fully understand their motivations, which in turn will shed light upon the xenoforms they generate or control.

The Shapers

"Out of the bog arose a great, mossy thing like a boulder, as big around as a dining table. It rose slowly into the air; from its underside hung a tangle of what appeared to be long, ropy vines, dripping brackish water and bits of half-eaten fish and other small creatures. The ends of these vines dragged limply in the marsh grass as the thing floated in my direction. Then the tentacles—for that's what they were, I now realized—began to stir, their ends groping blindly toward me, hungrily. And a mighty 'presence' entered my head. I don't know what else to call it. I stood there gaping at the creature as it approached, sickened by the pressure in my head, nearly helpless. I couldn't break free, couldn't lift my flamer. But by summoning every bit of my resolve, I managed to fire it at the ground between us. As the blazing fuel washed toward the thing, I felt the presence draw back in startlement, and I fled.

"But ever since, I've felt the presence in the back of my mind, whispering. And when I sleep, the thing appears in my dreams, calling me. It's driving me mad!"

General Description: The ancestors of the Shaper race were most certainly aquatic. In physical form, a Shaper consists primarily of a large (5-10 m³) shell containing the creature's internal organs, as well as numerous gas bladders for buoyancy in water. Projecting through small (roughly 2 cm diameter) holes in the shell's sides and bottom are multiple long (2-3 m), prehensile tentacles. These tentacles are incapable of fine manipulation; instead they are used primarily to draw food (animal and vegetable) into a platter-sized oral orifice on the shell's under surface.

But the Shaper race is highly developed psy-

Chapter 9: Nonplayer Characters

chically. Shapers are able to levitate objects by the power of their minds, and self-levitation has granted them the means of locomotion necessary to leave their native oceans and become an amphibious race. It was their other psychic abilities, however, that elevated the Shapers to sapient status and lead them to predominance among the stars. That is, having been denied the physical means by which to develop tools and rise to intelligence, the Shapers learned to use their psychic powers to manipulate other life forms. Specifically, they are able to psychically sense and control lesser creatures, using them as surrogate eyes through which to see, surrogate hands by which to build, plant, herd, and make war. In this manner, the early Shapers progressed from fledgling, Stone Age communities to a galactic civilization.

Along the way, they learned to refine their psychic manipulation to the point of guiding the genetic development of subject races, producing ever more evolved servants. Eventually, they even learned to effect genetic changes within individual subjects, allowing them to mutate those creatures into specialized agents over the course of relatively short periods of time.

It is only natural, then, that the Shapers have depended so heavily upon specifically bred biological "weaponry" during the course of their war with the Artificers. They sent swarms of tailor-made assassins after their enemies' colonies in specially-designed living starships. To deny the Artificers other bases, they modified the ecosystems of entire worlds, creating living hells of them . . . when time permitted. When it did not, they seeded those planets with carnivorous creatures specially bred for their bloodthirstiness and durability, thereby dooming millions of innocent native species to extinction.

Shaper Tech: Nearly any sort of device used by humans has a Shaper analog, from flashlights to starships. But whereas human devices are usually electrical and/or mechanical in nature, Shaper devices are generally biological. For instance, Shaper flashlights are actually biolumi-nescent creatures that require feeding rather than battery replacement. By the same token, Shaper starships are huge, hollow creatures with a shell durable enough to withstand the rigors of space and to contain an interior atmosphere, with large, photo-opaquing viewports, and with other, specialized symbiotes inside to serve as controls and sensors, etc. Obviously, Shaper starships and other such creatures take considerable time and effort to create.

But not all Shaper devices are biological in nature. Where necessary, electro-mechanical devices are constructed as well. Upon first leaving their native oceans ages ago, the Shapers encountered several species of small primates similar to Terran spider monkeys—the surrogate hands by which they came to build their earliest civilizations and by which they still build machines where biotechnology will not serve. Over the millennia, the Shaper race has developed such a sense of familiarity with the Servants, as the primates are called, that each Shaper has come to view its Servants as extensions of itself. Because of this, the Servants have survived the ages with very little genetic change imposed by their masters. However, this symbiosis is less than truly ideal, where the development of electro-mechanical technologies are concerned. The Servants have no real intelligence of their own whereby they can invent or develop such devices, and the Shapers' inclination toward biotechnologies has left them considerably less adept at electro-mechanical ones. Consequently, while such things as hyperspace drives are electro-mechanical, they tend to be much bulkier than necessary (although still more powerful than human ones). They also have a disconcerting tendency to look more biological than geometrical, given the Shaper habit of using organic materials.

PC Encounters: By far, most Shaper-related encounters your PCs will have will be with deadly creatures left on various worlds to deny possession of those planets to the Artificers. Some of those creatures are described among

Chapter 9: Nonplayer Characters

the xenoforms below, enough to keep your PCs busy for some time, and you are encouraged to invent more. Pretty much any sort of nasty creatures you can think of will be appropriate.

If you decide to have your PCs encounter a Shaper itself, they will first come across its Servants and other such creatures that it keeps close at hand for immediate use. One great adventure possibility is to assume that an individual Shaper has been stranded on a colony world or has somehow made its way to Earth and is now mutating local flora and fauna to suit its own purposes, those being: 1) to survive, 2) to study nearby humans, and 3) to enslave or destroy those humans, depending on the results of those tests. The PCs are called in to investigate a rash of mutated wildlife; this leads them into battles with enslaved and malformed humans. Once they track the Shaper to its lair, they must combat a band of tool-wielding monkey-like creatures (the Servants) before ultimately discovering and confronting the Shaper itself.

Typical Statistics, Shaper:

Fit: 65	Lea: 80	Psy: 85	Cha: 05
Ref: 20	Int: 85	Wil: 65	Pos: NA
Stamina: 32	Body: 16		

Movement: Shapers move at normal human speeds.

Other Notes: The shell of a Shaper gives the creature a natural armor that lowers any damage done to it by 4 points, as well as reducing lethality ratings by 3. The oral cavity provides the only significant entry through the armor and into the vital organs within.

Besides levitating objects weighing up to 150 kg and using them to make physical attacks (e.g., dropping a boulder on an enemy's head or whipping glass shards into a potentially lethal whirlwind), Shapers are capable of making direct psychic attacks. A Willpower roll is required to succeed, and the attack damage is 3d8(2). Stamina points lost by the victim of such an attack represent shock; body point loss is due to cranial hemorrhaging.

Mutation caused by a Shaper's psychic manipulation of a creature's genes takes some time to become physically evident, of course, as old (normal) cells die off and new (mutated) cells replace them. Hair, nails, and skin can change within just a few days; organ or skeletal mutation requires weeks or months. All three may be occurring at the same time.

Typical Statistics, Servant:

Fit: 20	Lea: 05	Psy: 10	Cha: 55
Ref: 75	Int: 15	Wil: 15	Pos: NA
Stamina: 9	Body: 5		

Movement: Servants move at 1.5 times normal human speeds.

Other Notes: There are usually 2d6 Servants present per Shaper. These creatures attack as humans and are able to use whatever equipment the controlling Shaper understands. Because of their relatively small size, however, they do one less point of damage than normal in all hand-to-hand attacks.

The Artificers

"Okay, here's my report:

"My squad was sent over the crater wall on foot, to recon what had shot down the survey skimmer. The original orbital survey of this moon had revealed no signs of xenological artifacts, and according to the mining corp's satellites nothing unidentified had come in-system since that time. As you can imagine, then, the bigwigs were hot to find out just what had fired that beam. So there we were, sweating along in full vacuum combat gear, toting laser rifles because of the vacuum and climbing a wall that was way too steep and way too tall for my liking.

"I led the squad to a point on the rim close to where the satellite had marked the beam's origin. From the cover there, we peered down the slope of the inner wall. And there, about a hundred meters away, was a long, rough trench stretching halfway across the crater floor. We could see the rear of some sort of space craft

Chapter 9:
Nonplayer Characters

sticking out at one end of the trench; the rest was buried under all the rock and dust it'd plowed up in its passage. What we could see of the thing looked pretty busted up; from the size, I'd guess it was some sort of escape pod.

"Jackson was on point. I signalled for radio silence, then gestured him forward, and he went over and down in a zigzag pattern, expecting any second to get fried, I'm sure. But he wasn't. From the trench's edge just behind the craft, he motioned a cautious advance, and I led the rest of the squad forward.

"It was definitely an alien ship. I saw what appeared to be a gun mount on its hull and had Juarez blow it away with her sniper laser. The researchers back at the base would be ticked, I knew, but they weren't in its line of fire. Jackson went into the trench, sidling toward a hatch below the ruined gun mount. But before he got there a panel opened next to the hatch and something that looked like an antenna poked out. It shot him to pieces with some sort of beam weapon before he could so much as blink; he was dead before he hit the ground. The squad responded by drilling the thing with their lasers, and I don't just mean the antenna: that hatchway looked like a sieve by the time we were done with it.

"I entered the ship. It was pretty much all cockpit inside. There were two cushioned couch-things. One was empty. On the other lay this multi-limbed space suit, like some giant caterpillar. It had a bubble helmet at one end, the interior surface all molded over with some sort of fungus. Apparently the creature inside had died in, or prior to, the vessel's crash, but the suit's integrity had held long enough for it to rot. Some of the rounds we'd fired into the hatchway had torn the suit up a bit, though; I caught glimpses of an odd-looking skeleton inside. Apparently, a couple of rounds had hit the control panels, too. They were a bit scorched.

"You want me to say I'm sorry? One of my guys died out there. We did what we had to do."

General Description: As deadly enemies of the Shapers, the Artificers are as skilled in electro-mechanical workings as the Shapers are in the biological.

In form, an Artificer consists of a fleshy, three-to four-meter long torso with an interior skeleton, sprouting six to 10 paired limbs, and surmounted by a bony head. The face consists of a ring of eight spider-like eyes above a long, stiff, sharp proboscis. Artificers are carnivores, using this proboscis to drool or inject digestive juices onto or into their prey, then suck up the liquified results.

Each of an Artificer's limbs end in a hand of three completely opposable digits, allowing the creature to grasp and manipulate large, complicated, and/or multiple objects. Those limbs nearest the creature's head are the most delicate and dexterous, those near its tail the strongest and heaviest. Typically, an Artificer stands on all but its foremost two pairs of limbs, but it can stand on fewer to provide more hands for a task. When necessary, it can even rear up on the last two pairs alone and hunch its upper body like a great question mark in order to bring all other hands to bear on one bit of work.

The inherent manipulative abilities of the Artificers, together with their aggressiveness as carnivores and their relative physical fragility, propelled the race toward expertise as tool-users early in their evolution. Once set on the road to mechanical development, the Artificers pursued that course with abandon. By the time of their disastrous first contact with the Shapers, they had developed such technological expertise as to build extremely fast starships, powerful long-range beam weapons, and even a nearly autonomous race of robot servants.

Obviously, the Shapers saw the Artificers as a dangerous competitor for the stars, and the two began warring almost at first contact. The Shapers posed their superior numbers and greater adaptability to new worlds against the superior ships and weapons of the Artificers, and the Ancients' War was begun in earnest.

Chapter 9:
Nonplayer Characters

Artificer Tech: The Artificers can serve as the source of pretty much any type of robotic opponent you want to send your PCs up against. Tiny insectoid assassination machines, incredibly realistic androids, cybernetic starships capable of pursuing other vessels through hyperspace—all have been built by the Artificers at one time or another and are lurking about for your PCs to encounter.

One design assumption we make is that cybernetics are considerably less space-efficient than organic brains. Consequently, the smaller the robot, the less intelligent it can be. Crab-sized assassination robots, for instance, have a very limited programming and can be outwitted fairly easily by anyone aware of their presence. Full-sized androids—with a torso full of cybernetic circuitry—have a much broader repertoire of behaviors and may even be expert in particular skills, but they are still less than human in terms of overall intelligence, however realistic they might look. Robots the size of a combat tank or small starship approach human intelligence; larger ones might even surpass it a bit. But it is important to realize that intelligence and knowledge (information storage) are not the same thing. While organic sapience has the edge in terms of intelligence, electro-mechanical robots have a distinct advantage in terms of capacity for storage of information. What this means is that robots—especially those approaching human size, or larger—have a very great deal more sheer memory than do individual people.

By way of illustration, let us suppose that an android were pursuing a lone human through an orbital factory complex. By accessing the complex's central computer, the android could, within moments, record to memory the design specifications of the complex, thereby knowing the location of every hatch, every corridor, every vent, every power line, and the function of every machine, every indicator light, etc., in the complex—something no human could hope to do, even given months of study. On the other hand,

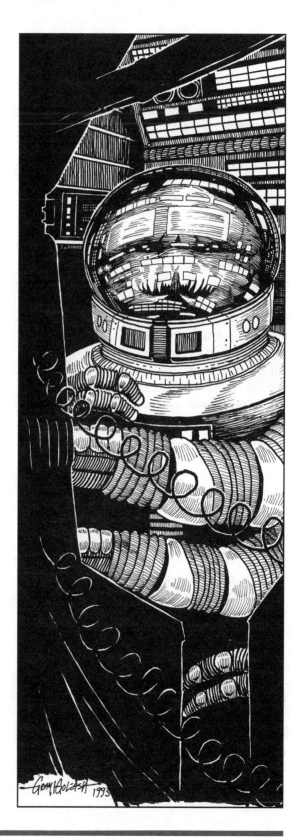

Chapter 9:
Nonplayer Characters

the human, being much more inventive, could extrapolate unexpected ways of using the equipment at hand, luring the android into deadly traps or otherwise tricking it.

Of course, robots are not all that the Artificers have constructed. Like humans, they have made all sorts of mechanical and electrical tools and devices, from mallets and ground vehicles to holographic projectors and starships. The PCs might find any or all such stuff abandoned on other worlds or still in the possession of an Artificer. One thing to keep in mind, however, is that while the function of such devices will be similar to human ones, their appearance will be considerably different, reflecting an alien aesthetic. Whereas human machines tend to consist of flat planes, rods, and cylinders, Artificer constructs tend toward segmented bulbous shapes augmented by spikes and spirals. Consequently, when the PCs run across such devices, they will have to do some (potentially dangerous) experimentation to determine what function they perform.

Chrysalis: Obviously, not every device created by the Artificers has a human analog. The Chrysalis, a form of containment device, is one example of a truly alien item. A small pellet about 15 mm in diameter, it stuns any victim it strikes and immediately begins to create a polygonal crystalline enclosure, surrounding the individual completely. One chrysalis can enclose a being of up to three meters in height.

A chrysalis is not affected by pounding, hammering, sawing, drilling, clawing, or other common physical attacks. A high-intensity sonic blast is the most effective tactic to use against one of these cages, causing it to shatter.

PC Encounters: Encounters with Artificers themselves will be even rarer than those with Shapers. Typically, rather than encountering an Artificer, the PCs will discover facilities that the race once populated. This might be such things as a factory still staffed by robots, a robotic mining vehicle, an automated starship patrolling old lines of commerce, or even an abandoned colony. On a lifeless world, such a site could be protected by a central computer controlling the facility's functions, locking the PCs into corridor sections and evacuating the atmosphere, filling the area with poison gas, electrifying the floor, or what-not. On living worlds, Artificer facilities might be protected, at least in part, by robotic "guard dogs" or tiny hunter-killer robots with poison injectors. Extremely important facilities, such as military bases, might even have weapon systems built into the walls.

When humanity comes to the attention of the Artificers in your campaign, the aliens could very well send androids to infiltrate and study the human race, perhaps even on Earth itself. In order to enhance their chances of passing as human, such androids would likely be remotely controlled (or at least advised) from a hidden cybernetic spacecraft, itself protected by smaller patrol 'bots and impressive weapons systems.

When the PCs encounter an actual Artificer, it should be because the thing is involved in some mission so important as to require its hands-on attention. And, of course, it will be even more heavily protected than the most impressive of the race's robotic agents.

Typical Statistics:

Fit: 35	Lea: 85	Psy: 15	Cha: 05
Ref: 65	Int: 60	Wil: 40	Pos: NA
Stamina: 19	Body: 9		

Movement: The Artificers move at normal human speed.

Chapter 9:
Nonplayer Characters

Xenoforms

Besides the Ancients and their creations, there have been numerous other life forms within humanity's region of the galaxy, many of them sapient. During the course of the Ancients' War, many have been brought to extinction, leaving only ruins to tell of their passing, while others were scattered among various solar systems, sent on one mission or another and then abandoned when their usefulness had come to an end.

The following, then, are sample xenoforms that your PCs may encounter during their missions to the stars. They can be placed as needed to serve your adventures.

Arachenoid

An arachenoid is an example of a tiny robot built to hunt and kill. In combat, it scuttles rapidly across the ground and can leap up to three meters vertically from a standstill. Its only attack form is injection of a deadly poison doing 4d6 on the initial turn.

Typical Statistics:
Fit: 30   Lea: NA   Psy: 60   Cha: NA
Ref: 60   Int: 10   Wil: 10   Pos: NA
Stamina: 10   Body: 7
Movement: Arachenoids move at 1.5 times human speed.

Assassinoid

This murder machine is an example of a fully human-looking android, with near-human intelligence and greater-than-human durability. Because of its great strength, an assassinoid does triple damage with all hand-to-hand and thrown weapon attacks. In addition, its tough build acts as armor blocking up to 15 points of damage per attack and reducing lethality ratings by 6 points.

Assassinoids are intelligent enough to hide within human society, but they must be programmed ahead of time with the appropriate culture and with a specific mission. While they are inventive enough to formulate minor changes to that mission plan as necessary, any major difficulties will leave them confused and uncertain as to how best to proceed.

Because they are relatively difficult to produce, there are limited numbers of assassinoids in existence at this time. This is fortunate, as in large numbers these androids could conceivably destroy all of human civilization.

Typical Statistics:
Fit: 95   Lea: 30   Psy: 75   Cha: 30
Ref: 90   Int: 35   Wil: 85   Pos: NA
Stamina: 90   Body: 47
Movement: Assassinoids move at 1.5 times human speed. They never tire.

Assimilator

The assimilator is a particularly hideous creature that grows by capturing other beings and grafting them onto itself to create a sort of horrible colony of linked but distinct consciousnesses. It assimilates its victim's limbs and organs into a hodgepodge overall network, leaving these victims with their sense of self intact but helplessly enslaved to the colony mind.

As a result, the composite creature is vaguely mound-like in shape, with limbs and heads at least partially protruding in nearly every direction. In combat, when the central brain is too busy to repress them, the creature emits a continuous chorus of tortured moans from its member parts.

Besides being able to do multiple separate melee attacks per turn—one for every 10 body points it possesses, at 2d4(1) damage each (more if armed with hand-to-hand weapons)—the assimilator is so horrible a sight that all who view it must make a Willpower test each turn to avoid fleeing in panic. Once a victim has been rendered unconscious from loss of stamina points, it can be assimilated within 1d6x10 minutes, adding half its Fitness and Willpower to the

Chapter 9:
Nonplayer Characters

creature's whole. The victim can be rescued during this time frame, but tearing the victim loose from the composite creature causes one point of body damage per minute spent being assimilated.

There is virtually no limit as to how big an assimilator can grow by co-opting other creatures into itself.

Typical Statistics:

Fit: 75   Lea: 50   Psy: 90   Cha: NA
Ref: 50   Int: 65   Wil: 45   Pos: NA
Stamina: 30   Body: 19

Movement: The Assimilator moves at normal human speeds.

Goo

This is simply a large (five-meter diameter) blob of protoplasm that attacks by enveloping its victims, who suffer from suffocation and acid (digestive juices) damage equal to 4d8 per turn engulfed. A victim who passes a Fitness test can avoid the suffocation, reducing the damage to 3d8. A victim can wrestle free from the goo entirely by passing a second Fitness check, taking only 2d4 damage in the process.

The goo itself takes no damage from normal attacks and can only be injured by explosions (half damage), fire (normal damage), or freezing (which crystallizes it).

Typical Statistics:

Fit: 90   Lea: NA   Psy: 80   Cha: NA
Ref: 30   Int: NA   Wil: 90   Pos: NA
Stamina: 44   Body: 22

Movement: Goo moves at ½ human speeds.

Hell Hound

This is a sleek, black hunting creature something like a spiky panther. It has an extremely high metabolism, which makes it capable of incredible running speed but also keeps it perpetually hungry. The spines across its skull and along its back ooze an irritant substance which makes the creature somewhat difficult to attack in hand-to-hand combat. Blows that miss the creature and exceed a failure margin rating of F8 result in the attacker being pricked by a spine for 2d4 (1) damage, plus 2d6 (3) from the poison.

The hell hound attacks twice with teeth and claws each round for 3d6 (4) damage per attack.

Typical Statistics:

Fit: 60   Lea: NA   Psy: NA   Cha: NA
Ref: 80   Int: NA   Wil: 60   Pos: NA
Stamina: 30   Body: 15

Movement: A hell hound moves at double human speeds.

Hell's Hornet

This is a small (one meter tall), quick, and deadly animal that looks vaguely like a cross between a monkey and a hornet. Its four spidery limbs and double pair of gliding wings sprout from a segmented body covered with bony plates and bristling with stiff black hair.

In combat, the creature attacks with fangs and claws for 2d8(2) damage or uses its ovipositor to inject a paralyzing poison (the puncture itself does 2d4(1) damage). The ovipositor attack is at a –20 penalty to hit but injects a poison that reduces the victim's Reflexes rating by 10 points per turn, with the victim becoming completely paralyzed when Reflexes reach 0.

The Hornet is carnivorous, subsisting on rodent-sized animals, birds, insects, and worms. After mating with another of its kind (the creatures are hermaphroditic), it reproduces by implanting a single, fist-sized egg deep within the abdomen of a paralyzed, human-sized host. The egg hatches within three days, at which point the larvae begins consuming the host (resulting in death within a few minutes). Three days later, upon finishing its meal, the larvae has reached the size of a human toddler, and it cocoons itself. Another three days later, it

Chapter 9:
Nonplayer Characters

emerges as a miniature adult. Within two weeks of intensive hunting and eating, it has reached full adult size and is ready to produce its own offspring.

Humans are just beginning to encounter these creatures on Acey-Two, where the major southern continent has an infestation in its tropical forests.

Typical Statistics:

Fit: 30   Lea: NA   Psy: 80   Cha: NA
Ref: 75   Int: NA   Wil: 50   Pos: NA
Stamina: 20   Body: 7

Movement: The Hell's Hornet moves at 1.5 times human speed on the ground and glides at double human speed.

Hunters

Perhaps the most dangerous of all the beings created by the Shapers is a deadly creature of rudimentary intelligence, considerable cunning, and incredible adaptability, typically called a Hunter by those minor races unfortunate enough to know of its existence.

General Description: In a fully relaxed state in its natural oceanic habitat, a Hunter is a large (slightly greater than human-sized) amorphous blob of protoplasm. But the creature is seldom in such a state of relaxation. It has incredible control over the shape and density of its own body, to the extent that it is able to form specialized organs at will. It can toughen its exterior to form a durable integument, create sensory organs of various types, extrude limbs and reabsorb them, even create an exo- or endoskeletal system for short periods of time. In fact, the specialized configurations that Hunters are able to develop are limited only by an individual's inventiveness (to conceive of a new type of organ or to discover how to mimic one, once observed) and force of will (to physically create the structure and to maintain that structure's shape, once it has been formed). Experienced Hunters might even be able to pass themselves off as human

from a distance, though the likeness would be rough, and they would be hard pressed to master multiple details at once, such as body hair, teeth, and nails.

Hunters are so named because of their delight in stalking and killing other creatures; they have been designed to do so as violently and cruelly as possible.

Effects of Damage: In combat, a Hunter can suffer severe damage with no visible effect other than a diminishing of mass caused by the loss of stamina points (Hunters have no body point rating) and the possibility of reverting to its natural form (due to a loss of concentration).

Mass Effects: Cuts and stab wounds to a Hunter simply seal over without inflicting any real damage. Gunshot wounds and the like cause normal damage and decrease the creature's mass proportionately. But all attack types are considered to have a lethality rating of 0 versus Hunters, even system-wide attacks such as immolation, electrical shock, and poison. Although these attacks cause normal damage, the creature simply sheds its destroyed cells.

To determine the visible results of a Hunter's loss of mass because of damage, simply compare the number of damage points inflicted to the number of stamina points remaining to the creature, then deduct this same percentage from the creature's current mass.

For example, a Hunter with 100 stamina points which suffered 10 points of damage would lose 10% of its mass. If it were configured as a 180 cm-tall humanoid at the time, it would lose roughly 18 cm (10%) of that height. Alternatively, the GM might choose to have it stay the same height but lose some body part (arm, head, etc.), depending on the attack.

As the creature grows smaller from such mass reduction, keep in mind that it should do slightly less damage in combat. A good rule of thumb is to impose a penalty of –1 to its damage rolls for each 20 percent of original mass lost.

Willpower Checks: Whenever a Hunter loses more than 20% of its current stamina points in a

Chapter 9:
Nonplayer Characters

single turn, it must roll versus Willpower to retain its assumed shape, subtracting the amount of damage just suffered from its Willpower. If the Hunter fails this roll, it immediately reverts to protoplasmic form for the rest of the turn. During its initiative point on the following turn, it can resume its former shape or assume another by passing an unmodified Willpower roll.

By the same token, a Hunter must make a Willpower check each time it wants to change form during combat, whether it be something as simple as sprouting claws or as difficult as changing body shape entirely. If the check is failed, the Hunter cannot change its form that turn.

Shape Abilities: Exactly what adaptive feats an individual Hunter can accomplish is up to you, as GM, but the following special abilities can serve as a sampling of possibilities.

Enhanced Senses: This option covers a wide range of possibilities: eagle-like sight, bat-like hearing, wolf-like sense of smell, radio-wave reception, etc.

Armor Skin: The Hunter is able to form an extremely durable outer layer of skin, capable of resisting 5 points of damage in combat and of protecting the creature from double that amount of fire or vacuum damage.

Bony Club: This is a blunt, heavy limb used for smashing attacks. It does damage as a club.

Entanglement: The creature creates tentacles or net-like webbed extremities to entrap foes.

Claws/Blades: This represents the ability to sprout fangs, claws, spikes, or actual blades, typically on a jaw or an extremity but sometimes as a porcupine-like defense on a shell over the torso. Treat as a knife, machete, or spear.

Stink: The creature may produce a cloud of gas capable of stunning (like a stun grenade) or nauseating all those within its area who fail a Fitness check at –30. Nauseated characters suffer an Initiative penalty of –5 in combat and perform all skill tests at –20.

Shriek: The Hunter may produce a blast of sound so loud and shrill that all within the area

Chapter 9:
Nonplayer Characters

are automatically deafened for 2d4 turns and stunned for half that time unless they pass a Fitness test. See Stink, above, for sample effects of the stun.

Electrical Shock: The Hunter shares with several native Terran creatures the ability to generate electrical potential within its body and then stun a victim with it. The Hunter's shock does 3d8 damage to its target upon contact and stuns the victim for the duration of the combat turn (i.e., the victim loses the chance to act in that turn).

Poison: Creating a poison requires more than simply reconfiguring shape; specialized organs must be developed and chemical changes made within them. For that reason, few Hunters know how to do it.

Typical Hunter poison does 3d6 points of damage on the first turn.

Acid Spray: Instead of injecting poison into a victim, a Hunter may spit acid. Damage is treated the same as for poison.

Typical Statistics:

Fit: 80	Lea: NA	Psy: 60	Cha: 05
Ref: 75	Int: 15	Wil: 70	Pos: NA
Stamina: 100	Body: NA		

Movement: Hunter movement rates are variable, depending upon current body configuration. In their natural form, they move at half human speeds.

Nestling

Nestlings are tiny creatures resembling a furry soccer ball on legs with a wide mouth full of sharp fangs. At night, they travel in packs like land-born piranhas, swarming over whatever animal they can catch and stripping the meat from its bones within minutes, biting for 2d10(2) damage each.

Fortunately, the things have a strong aversion to light and tend to huddle together in a safe place—typically a hastily dug burrow—during daylight hours.

Typical Statistics:

Fit: 10	Lea: NA	Psy: 66	Cha: 70
Ref: 65	Int: 15	Wil: 15	Pos: NA
Stamina: 6	Body: 2		

Movement: Nestlings move at double human speeds.

Quarm

These bipedal reptiles at one time had an advanced civilization that was beginning to explore its own solar system. Then they were discovered by the Shapers and pressed into service as troops in the Ancients' War. Now most suffer savage living conditions, surviving in Stone Age squalor on various primitive worlds where they were abandoned by their masters. They retain legends of their former level of cultural development, however, and they bide their time, waiting for the opportunity to regain what they have lost. Some of these legends predict the coming of another race as saviors, legends that the PCs could benefit from if their trigger fingers aren't too twitchy upon first encountering these "savages."

The Quarm are somewhat larger (2.5 meters tall), bulkier (averaging 150 kg), and slower than humans, but they are also stronger and tougher. In combat, they add 2d3 damage to all their hand-to-hand and thrown weapon attacks due to this high strength. In addition, their leathery skin acts as armor, stopping 4 points of damage on each attack and lowering lethality ratings by 2.

Typical Statistics:

Fit: 85	Lea: 35	Psy: 65	Cha: 55
Ref: 55	Int: 60	Wil: 80	Pos: NA
Stamina: 55	Body: 28		

Movement: Quarm move at 3/4ths the normal human rates.

Chapter 9:
Nonplayer Characters

Tazzim

The Tazzim are another race co-opted into the Ancients' War as soldiers, this time by the Artificers. As such, they developed an antipathy for the Quarm that they are having a difficult time overcoming, despite their intellectual realization that the Quarm had as little choice in the matter as they. Whereas the Quarm were forced to resort to a savage lifestyle upon being abandoned by the Shapers, the Tazzim managed to escape the Artificers' hold and flee with some of that race's technological artifacts. Now they live like stellar nomads, constantly on the move (to avoid being recaptured) in rattletrap starships that they keep in operation only by luck and stubbornness.

In form, the Tazzim are mere meter-tall bipeds descended from feline-like ancestors. What they lack in mass, however, they more than make up for in inventiveness, camaraderie, and agility.

In hand-to-hand combat, they do 1 point less damage than normal for humans. But they gain a +10 modifier to all ranged attacks, due to their natural agility.

Like the Quarm, the Tazzim could become friends of the PCs, should they be approached in the right way.

Typical Statistics:

Fit: 30	Lea: 70	Psy: 75	Cha: 70
Ref: 80	Int: 75	Wil: 50	Pos: NA
Stamina: 15	Body: 5		

Wraither

These slim, pale, and timid humanoids were well on their way to colonizing the stars when they first encountered the Ancients and their war. The Wraithers avoided becoming embroiled in that war by scattering themselves among the barren places of the galaxy—airless moons, tiny asteroids, and dead planets circling inhospitable stars—and retreating far underground. In those tunnels and caverns, they maintain a highly technological existence, but one devoted entirely to peace.

The Wraithers are quite human in appearance, though a bit more frail, and with larger heads and eyes. Should the PCs encounter them, the Wraithers will do what they can to escape actual contact, but continually peaceful gestures may win them over. They could become valuable allies, as the Wraithers represent the Terrans' best chance to learn the history behind the Ancients' War. However, no Wraither will ever join into a fight, no matter what the provocation. The Wraithers believe it better to die than to kill.

Typical Statistics:

Fit: 35	Lea: 95	Psy: 80	Cha: 70
Ref: 55	Int: 90	Wil: 40	Pos: NA
Stamina: 18	Body: 7		

Terrans

A number of standard human types will show up regularly in BUGHUNTERS™ adventures. We offer you the following sampling of particularly significant NPC roles.

UTRPF Officer

All full officers in UTRPF are human, of course, and this puts some strain on relations between them and their synner troops. In general, the range of feelings these officers have toward the troops they command runs from grudging admiration to imperiousness as a cover for fear or hatred. In any event, however, officers are likely to watch synners closely, question their every decision, doubt any conclusions or recommendations they make, and otherwise generally cause the PCs to feel like second-class citizens. After all, that's their job.

Typical Statistics:

Fit: 60	Lea: 60	Psy: 60	Cha: 60
Ref: 60	Int: 50	Wil: 50	Pos: 75
Stamina: 27	Body: 15		

Chapter 9:
Nonplayer Characters

Groundling

"Groundling" is the term synners and colonists commonly use for civilians who never leave the Earth. The typical groundling attitude toward synners is ambivalent, a mixture of gratitude with racism, but there exist a number of synners' rights activists who can be of great help, as may donors' families and friends.

Typical Statistics:

Fit: 35	Lea: 50	Psy: 40	Cha: 50
Ref: 40	Int: 55	Wil: 45	Pos: 40
Stamina: 20	Body: 8		

Colonist

Most colonists are made of more durable stuff than the average human, both mentally and physically. In addition, the majority have some sort of skill that makes them desirable as colonists, so that United Terra is willing to choose them above other hopeful citizens.

Colonists usually have a more open attitude toward synners than other humans do. This is because frontier living tends to draw individualists and makes people respected more for their actions than for their backgrounds. Also, a colonist is more likely than the average groundling to have seen synners in action and thus to have a clear idea of how much they owe to them.

Typical Statistics:

Fit: 60	Lea: 55	Psy: 50	Cha: 55
Ref: 55	Int: 65	Wil: 60	Pos: 45
Stamina: 30	Body: 15		

Chapter 10:
Sample Adventures

The adventure potential of the BUGHUNTERS™ game milieu is enormous, and as UTRPF synths, player characters are perfectly positioned to experience it all.

For one thing, as synthetic humans, the PCs will often serve as or on a starship crew, because of their ability to remain awake during hyperspace travel. As a glance through this chapter will reveal, there are multiple events and plots that can occur during their voyages, leading to adventures that are all the more horrific and exciting because of the isolation inherent in such travel.

Of course, the worlds of humanity's extrasolar colonies and outposts are nearly as isolated. Even the largest and longest established of them have very small populations and extremely limited resources in comparison to the Lunar and Martian colonies, being so much farther removed from Earth. As the PCs shuttle colonists and deliver supplies to these remote locations, they will have ample opportunity to encounter the strange alien life forms of those worlds, as well as hideous creatures planted there unnaturally. And, certainly, the colonists themselves have private goals and schemes of their own, in which the PCs, in their role as United Terra's peacekeepers, will often find themselves embroiled.

On occasion, the PCs will also be assigned as explorers of new stellar systems, beyond the reaches of previous missions. Besides the natural hazards of such exploration, here the PCs may encounter beastly, blood-thirsty creatures, discover the ruins of alien civilizations, perhaps even stumble across the refugee remnants of a minor race that has been driven to the edge of extinction in the Ancients' War—survivors whose reaction to the PCs may range from cautious stalking to panicked violence. On one such expedition the PCs might encounter one of the Ancients themselves; they might even find themselves being used as pawns in one of the races' machinations against the other, or they may encounter other humans who have been cap-tured and "retooled" as Shaper warriors or replaced by Artificer Assassinoids.

But the PCs will not always be assigned to tasks outside the Solar System. Frequently, they will be cycled back home for R&R or for some special assignment. One such mission type that is rife with long-term campaign possibilities pits the PCs against alien infiltrators on Terra itself! This is why Chapter 1 included notes on player character interaction with their own donors—after all, if you can't trust "yourself," whom can you trust?

This is hardly an exhaustive list of BUGHUNTERS adventure possibilities, however. Many science-fiction movie, novel, and short story plots lend themselves easily to adaptation for the BUGHUNTERS milieu (see the suggested reading and viewing list on page 118 for a few recommendations). Clever Game Masters need not worry about ever running out of adventures.

Besides providing you with outlines for a few such sample adventures, this chapter will provide you with aids to help you make the most of your own adventure ideas.

Basic Premises

In designing BUGHUNTERS adventures for your campaign and incorporating those listed in this chapter, you should be aware of a few premises underlying the design of this game.

Typical Adventures

A standard BUGHUNTERS adventure plot runs something like this: 1) The PCs discover (somehow) the existence of some bugs. It may be accidentally, in the course of a routine assignment, or they may be sent specifically in response to reports. 2) They investigate to learn the extent of the threat. This may mean slogging through a swamp, questioning locals, hanging out in expectation of an attack, or whatever. 3) They come up with a plan to defeat the crea-

Chapter 10:
Sample Adventures

tures. Sometimes they may only have seconds to do so (in the face of a major attack, for instance); at others they may have days or more to prepare. 4) They have a climactic battle. 5) They go home to lick their wounds and receive their rewards.

Once that pattern has been established in your players' minds (after half a dozen such adventures, perhaps), you can extend the life of a campaign by beginning to play with the pattern, varying some of the elements.

For instance, you may begin playing with the concept of bug as enemy. The first time the PCs meet a minor alien race, for example, they will very likely expect them to be hostile, when the best result of the adventure would actually be to make peaceful contact. At the opposite end of the spectrum, you can surprise the players by having people who would normally be their allies, such as colonists, become the enemy under the mental domination of some force or another.

Similarly, you can reverse the normal "investigation-and-pursuit" process by having the PCs be on the receiving end once in a while. This may be as simple as setting them up in an overland trek somewhere, then have them dogged by an enemy who already knows of their existence. Or it might involve an infiltration of UTRPF by invaders from within, with the PCs as targets because they are virtually the only ones who know of the invasion.

In any case, such changes should only be made after a norm is established for adventures, at which time they add additional depth and breadth to a campaign.

Typical Campaigns

Just as BUGHUNTERS™ adventures have a recognizable standard shape, so do campaigns in the game. On the one hand, BUGHUNTERS adventures tend to be fairly discrete episodes in a character's life, each with a relatively distinct beginning, middle, and end. On the other hand, it is a good idea to overlap the episodes a bit by planting the seeds of later adventures during the course of earlier ones, and the campaign itself can have an overall plot interwoven throughout.

In terms of planting seeds, imagine that you intend to run an adventure in which the PCs' Isler Drive is taken over by an alien device and their starship jumped (in one incredibly long, remote-controlled hyperspace leap) to a hidden Artificer base. With that in mind, you can have their drive act up a bit during one or more preceding adventures (because their future hijackers are working to get a fix on it). This will accomplish two things. First, it will give them something extraneous to worry about during those earlier adventures, which allows you to misdirect their attention somewhat when desired. Second, it makes the Artificer adventure seem less of a *deus ex machina* when it occurs, because the PCs have had clues to its coming for some time (though they could have no idea as to those clues' significance).

Concerning an overall campaign plot, you needn't have one at all, but it can add an extra element of depth and purpose, particularly if you plan to eventually bring a campaign to closure. One plot that can work quite naturally could be called "Exploration and Return." In this plot, their first few adventures take the PCs to humanity's current outposts, where they begin to learn how deadly their part of the galaxy is. As they proceed through other adventures, they begin to discover the ruins of other intelligent races, meet a few survivors of them, and learn of the Ancients' war. They become drawn more deeply into that war, perhaps even being captured by one of the Ancients, maybe to be rescued by their alien friends. One way or another, the PCs learn that humanity has piqued the Ancients' interest, and they return to Earth to warn the human race and help protect it from an invasion, overt or covert.

Chapter 10:
Sample Adventures

Placing Adventures

In designing the BUGHUNTERS™ milieu, we have purposely left you, as GM, a lot of room in which to work. You will notice, for example, that while the star map includes all stars within 30 light years of Sol, only a very few of the nearest are covered in the timeline. Alpha Centauri is listed as having an Earth-like world (AC2 or "Acey-Two") and at least one other planet; Barnard's Star, Wolf 359, UV Ceti, Ross 154, and Ross 248 all have had outpost teams sent to them (though the last three have run into trouble), indicating that there are planets there as well. Everything else is left open for you to place worlds as you see fit. As a guide, the following assumptions help define the BUGHUNTERS universe: 1) roughly 50% of all stars have worlds circling them; 2) A-class stars are too hot to have much of anything circling them, even at great distances; 3) M-class stars are too cold to have livable worlds; and 4) G-class stars are more likely to have livable worlds than are F- and K-class ones.

Earth-like worlds will be highly prized as places for human colonies to be placed. But even cold, dead worlds or very hot ones can be useful as places for outposts or mining complexes. As the PCs adventure, keep in mind that UTSA will continue to plant new facilities on ever more distant worlds, so the PCs will have lots of new places to visit as time goes on.

Note that Earth-like does not mean *exactly* like Earth. We have established AC2 as slightly hotter, overall, for instance, and one of the adventures later in this chapter deals with a primarily oceanic world. By the same token, you can invent livable worlds that are primarily ice, desert, mountain, or any other type of terrain.

Finally, note that we have not identified home systems for any of the xenoforms listed Chapter 9: Nonplayer Characters. As central devices of the overall BUGHUNTERS milieu, the Shapers and Artificers have been designed to have bases wherever the GM believes necessary, but to have homeworlds so distant as to be unimportant to a campaign. If you choose to change this, just be aware that there is a danger that either the homeworld will prove to be too much for the PCs to survive, or, by some remarkable turn of events, the PCs will prove to be too much for the homeworld. In either case, your campaign is likely to die as a result. Other xenoforms may have virtually forgotten their own original homeworlds or may be living on its ravaged remains, whichever you believe to be more dramatically appropriate.

With these various things in mind as guides to a sense of verisimilitude, place your worlds, colonies, and outposts as needed to make your campaign work best.

Sample Adventures

On the pages that follow, we include a number of sample adventures for you to run. If you are an extemporaneous sort of GM, you may not need much preparation to run any of these. Each is explained in some detail and divided into likely scenes. But most GMs will want to flesh things out more fully before beginning, perhaps making up encounter maps for important locations, for instance, reviewing the special abilities of the bugs involved, and creating stats for NPCs likely to be met along the way.

The additional plot ideas listed after the main adventures are provided as a spur toward the creation of other, similar, scenarios.

Lab Rats Amok!

In this adventure, the PCs are relaxing back at Stargate when a pack of biological nightmares break out of a corporate laboratory on the station and begin running loose, putting the survival of the entire station at risk.

Background: Midas Corporation maintains a laboratory facility on Stargate's main ring, where it experiments with adapting Terran crops and livestock to grow on other worlds. Recently, a

Chapter 10:
Sample Adventures

corporate mining team on an inhospitable world with next-to-no native life discovered a cache of nearly a hundred leathery, softball-sized eggs and sent them back to UTSA for study. But suspecting that the eggs might yield valuable insights into how best to settle the world, and wanting their own scientists to have a head start in analyzing them, they also sent a dozen of the eggs back to Midas, hidden in a crate of processed ore.

Unfortunately, when the eggs were hatched out in the Midas lab at Stargate, the creatures inside proved cunning enough to escape their cages, and vicious enough to kill a couple of lab workers in the process (Nestlings would work well for this adventure). Midas Corp's security forces want to keep the situation hushed up, believing that the things are hiding somewhere inside the lab building and that they can safely be tracked down. But a scientist on staff is afraid that they have escaped into Stargate's subterranean labyrinth of maintenance tunnels.

Act I: While out of the UTRPF compound on an evening pass to enjoy the sights and sounds of Stargate's civilian sector, the PCs are approached by the worried scientist, who begins to explain that Midas Corp has some dangerous lab specimens running loose. Before this individual can go into any great detail, however, Midas Corp security forces show up and try to drag the scientist away.

There follows a show-down between the PCs and security people (neither side is armed). One way or another, word gets back to UTRPF.

Act II: After several hours of anxious waiting for authorization from Earth, UTRPF sends the PCs (perhaps with some NPCs) to stage a raid on the Midas Corp labs, using non-lethal weapons. Eventually, the corp's security forces come to realize that there is no sense in resisting further and surrender, allowing the synners to explore the building. In a basement locker room, they discover the messy remains of a dead man in a shower and signs that, after killing him, the creatures squeezed their way into the drain pipe leading into Stargate's underground tunnels.

Act III (climax): When the PCs report the creatures' escape, UTRPF HQ orders them to pursue the things into the underground. The Midas labs prove to have an accessway to those tunnels. If the players think to look for them, let the PCs find and confiscate a cache of slightly heavier weapons from the corp's security center.

Inside the underground, the PCs play cat and mouse with the creatures through a maze of passageways. The xenos prove adept at leading the PCs into traps, tearing wiring loose and dropping live ends toward the synners, luring them into crawlspaces where the PCs can be attacked individually, attacking in locations with risk of dangerous ricochets or crossfire, or at slippery spots with long drops—perhaps even ending in front of a speeding subway train. UTRPF responds to any radio reports of this canniness by sealing off the tunnels (with the PCs inside!) to avoid infestation elsewhere.

Once all exits are cut off, the PCs should eventually be able to find and kill all the xenos. If the PCs do not alert UTRPF to the danger or if they force open an escape route for themselves, some of the creatures may escape into other areas of the station, where they will hide and breed until the entire L-5 facility must eventually be evacuated.

Time Bomb on Acey-Two

In response to a distress call from humanity's closest and most significant extra-solar colony, the PCs are sent to investigate what new predator is slaughtering the local wildlife. But by the time they arrive, the scope of the threat has mushroomed dangerously.

Background: Acey-Two has been considered something of a paradise, with an ecology that suits humans well and nothing so dangerous as to threaten Terrans' existence there. But recently, members of a minor colony on the world's southern continent have begun finding large (human-sized) local wildlife dead and partially

Chapter 10: Sample Adventures

eaten, and they know of no local predator that could have done it. As the number of kills rises, they radio a distress call to New Austin, the major colony city on the northern continent, which relays it to Stargate via Isler Radio.

Act I: The PCs are ordered to travel to Acey-Two to investigate this mystery. They are assigned equipment as seems appropriate to hunting a large predator such as a tiger and are given a relatively fast ship, one that can make the journey in roughly two to three months' time.

Act II: Arriving at Acey-Two, the PCs find that they cannot raise a radio response from the southern village. If contacted, New Austin in the north explains that a volunteer team went by VTOL weeks ago to investigate the radio silence but never reported back; the colony's governor has forbidden anyone else to go, preferring to await the PCs' arrival.

Act III: When they reach the southern village, the PCs find its entire population lying about, dead and partially eaten, including all livestock sheep-sized and up, as well as the members of the New Austin rescue mission and their VTOL. From the position of the bodies, and the weapons lying about, it looks as if the colonists put up a considerable struggle.

Upon further investigation, they find minutes of a town meeting which talks about "things from the air, like hornets from hell, coming from the western hills" and "sending a hunting team to find the creatures' nest and exterminate them."

Act IV: Setting out through the woods in pursuit of the hunting party, the PCs are attacked by a group of Hell's Hornets (see pages 104-105). After fighting the creatures off, they come across the remains of the hunters, apparently killed while running *back toward the village* (they had found the cache of Hornets and were fleeing in horror, having dropped any heavy equipment that might slow them down).

Act V (climax): The PCs backtrack the hunters' footsteps and discover the alien cache. It is a vast, underground complex, filled with thousands upon thousands of glowing pedestals arranged around a central power plant, each pedestal bearing a single Hell's Hornet cocoon held in stasis. Except for the 50 or so outermost ones, that is; these are dark and contain empty cocoons. As the PCs take all this in, another dozen pedestals flicker toward extinction, and their cocoons begin to stir as the creatures within begin breaking out. To make matters worse, the PCs have to be careful when combating these things not to damage the facility.

If the PCs are not careful, they are likely to precipitate the power plant's demise. But if they are careful not to wreck any of the pedestals, they can investigate the power plant controls and may be able to learn that its decay is accelerating and that within a few hours Hornets will be waking faster than they can kill them.

The only real solution is to bomb the facility into oblivion. Of course, future colonists will still have to deal with those that escaped before the PCs arrived and are now dwelling in the wild.

The Ghost Ship

Victims of shipwreck in days of old could always hope to wash up on some hospitable shore. But starship crews stranded light years from the nearest planet have no such hope. That is why, when little things begin going wrong during an interstellar voyage, it's more than merely an inconvenience; it's a reason to fear.

Background: Hyperspace is not entirely empty, any more than normal space is. Consequently, it is sometimes possible for a vessel cycling through hyperspace to come to the attention of things dwelling there. What's more, the Shapers have seeded regions of hyperspace with hostile energy beings that are capable of invading a living body and possessing it, even a body in stasis. Like their masters, the Shapers, these hyperspace "spirits" are capable of telepathy and telekinesis (the latter only while in possession of a physical body). Using these abilities, they wreak havoc as they may, sometimes sim-

Chapter 10: Sample Adventures

ply destroying the ships they plague, at other times attempting to remain undetected until they can reach a world full of potential victims.

In this adventure, one such being takes possession of a colonist in stasis on the PCs' ship.

Act I: The PCs are assigned to transport a load of people from a colony or outpost back to Stargate. A team of UT ambassadors and their entourage would work well, or perhaps a group of corporate middle managers.

Just before they lift off, however, another transport ship approaches with new colonists. It travels through the system at Isler speeds, without slowing or changing course, and is broadcasting a distress signal. As the only rescue means available, the PCs are forced to pursue the ship, match courses with it, and space walk one of their number across to take control. Once on board, that person discovers that the entire synner crew is missing. There are signs of violence, but no one is left on board except the colonists, who are safely locked in stasis (or so the PCs think). It looks as if the synners simply went mad and did away with themselves, tossing themselves out the airlock in the process. The ship's log and any private diary entries have been erased from the ship's computers, leaving no record of the crew's last days. When the ship is returned to the planet and the stasised colonists are wakened, they have no answer for the mystery.

You may wish to plant this act at the beginning of some other adventure, then leave it as a mystery for a while, springing the rest of this adventure at a later date.

Act II: Pressed for time, the PCs must take their own load of people and head for Stargate. As they travel, they each have a nightmare of some ominous evil presence trying to take over their minds (this is due to the hyperspace entity's unsuccessful attempts to possess the PCs one by one).

Shortly after the nightmares stop, little things begin to go wrong with the ship's drives: wiring comes loose in an essential place; power is shut off to one or more drives at the auxiliary panels within the drive section itself, slowing the ship or throwing it off course; an NPC is accidently electrocuted in a bizarre mishap; etc. These are due to the entity's having taken control of a colonist and telekinetically lifting that person in and out of the stasis pod to sabotage and delay the ship until enough other entities can arrive to take complete control of it.

Act III (climax): With the right skills, the PCs may find the saboteur by noting fluctuations in the person's stasis field. If discovered, the possessed individual will desperately try to evade capture and destroy the ship. Otherwise, once enough colonists have been possessed, the PCs will find themselves fighting an eerie mutiny.

Assuming that the PCs make it back to Stargate, hyperspace experts can free the colonists from possession. The PCs may find themselves leading a mission back to the world of the rescued ship to deal with any possessed colonists there as well.

Roach Motel

Sometimes it is much tougher to get out of a situation than to get into it. Such is the case with the abandoned Artificer base in this sample minor race adventure.

Background: Over the millennia of their war with the Shapers, the Artificers built untold numbers of hidden bases, many of which were subsequently abandoned when the race retreated from an area. But even these abandoned bases were left with automatic defenses operational, in order that they might remain a thorn in the Shapers' side.

The base in this adventure consists of a vast underground complex, surmounted by a surface security facility (much like a castle's gatehouse). Humans have discovered the surface building, and the PCs are sent to explore it, ignorant of the automated deathtrap that it becomes to intruders. Fortunately, a colony of Wraithers (see the NPC chapter) has burrowed into the under-

Chapter 10: Sample Adventures

ground complex and are available to help the PCs in their hour of need. Unfortunately, however, their furtiveness makes the aliens seem assassins rather than saviors.

Act I: The PCs are assigned to lead an exploratory team into an abandoned alien building that has recently come to light on a world humans are colonizing. There should be plenty of NPCs along on this adventure to provide bug-fodder.

The first difficulty to be overcome is to gain entrance. From the outside, the building is a nearly featureless block of some unknown metal alloy, approximately 100 meters on a side and 10 meters tall, with a single, five-meter square doorway in one face. Next to the doorway is a single column of 13 buttons. The door opens if the prime numbered ones (1, 2, 3, 5, 7, 11, and 13) are pressed in exact sequence, but to no other stimulus. This allows intelligent creatures to discover how to open the door but keeps animals out.

Upon opening the door, the PCs find an antechamber, dimly lit by power from somewhere within. Once all of the PCs are inside (not necessarily all the NPCs—this is a plot device), the outer door slams shut and cannot be opened again. But an open door appears in the room's back wall, luring the group on.

Act II: The group proceeds ever deeper into the building, plagued by automated attacks. You may create a mazy map to serve as the interior, or simply describe turns and distances at random. The PCs have no real choice but to proceed along their single course.

The traps include such things as sudden laser fire across a corridor, pits that drop a character into a roaring furnace, blades that scythe across a doorway, glassy panels that seal off an individual to suffocate in greenish poison gas, and the like. Many are certain death, but even the minor ones can be crippling. Play at this point relies heavily on Psyche rolls (to notice a trap) and Reflexes rolls (to react to unnoticed ones). When PCs fail, choose some less lethal trap, have an NPC get in the way of the damage, have a Wraither encounter (see below), or simply have another panel fall, blocking the group from retreat. When the PCs succeed at their rolls, spring an absolutely deadly trap on an NPC. The goal here is to horrify the PCs without frustrating them and to set them up for the Wraither encounters.

Act III (climax): When the PCs' presence comes to the Wraither's attention, the aliens (who have learned to manipulate the gatehouse, though not how to shut it down) decide to lend a hand, but without actually making contact. Consequently, when a trap is about to fry a PC, it will malfunction for a critical second (a laser starts to glow, then dies, then finally fires, for instance), allowing the PC to escape certain death. Immediately thereafter, PCs who pass a Psyche roll catch a quick glimpse of a Wraither fleeing the area. The first time or two this happens, they are likely to think the Wraithers the masterminds of the complex, but eventually they should make the connection between these appearances and the traps they survived and realize that they have unknown allies.

After a dozen traps or so, the PCs find themselves out of the gatehouse and in a tunnel leading back to the surface. If they never fired on the Wraithers, one of these aliens will cautiously approach to make contact. This, of course, is the main reward of the adventure.

The Devil of the Deep Blue Sea

Exploration is an exciting occupation, but it can be dangerous. When the risks of a mission become too great for humans, they call for synners to take their place.

Background: A research team based on an island of a primarily oceanic planet has been running survey equipment to map the ocean floor. Recently, while mapping a particularly deep trench, they picked up the sonar outline of a starship-sized object that was not there before. UTRPF has decided to send a team of synners to

Chapter 10:
Sample Adventures

do an on-site investigation of the object. When the PCs arrive, they find it is an alien starship—Tazzim is suggested—the crew of which has fallen prey to an Assimilator (see the NPC chapter for details of these two xenoforms).

Act I: The PCs are run through a crash course in deep-sea diving (possibly including some virtual reality time, to give them points to burn on mission skill tests), then sent to the planet with a mini-sub in their ship's hold. They arrive and meet the island staffers, some of whom insist on going along (basically to give the Assimilator something to munch on later in the adventure).

Act II: In the water, on their way to the object, the PCs are attacked by a gigantic native predator that they must fend off or destroy. Eventually reaching the object, they find that it is a starship, that its hull is unbroken, and that there are abundant signs that it sank here fairly recently (i.e., only shortly before the island staffers discovered it).

Act III (climax): Their mission orders require them to investigate further, so the PCs enter the starship. An airlock maintains a breathable internal atmosphere. Inside, the starship appears to be abandoned. But as they explore further, the PCs are stalked by the Assimilator which has absorbed the crew (and thus has their knowledge of the ship's layout and operation). It was this creature that caused the ship to crash.

Once the PCs learn the creature's nature through seeing one of their companions annexed to its body, they should realize that they can't afford to let it escape. Ideally, they set the starship's fusion drives to explode where they will vaporize the craft and its horrible occupant, then escape in their minisub.

Other Adventure Ideas

Adventures Near Home: Occasionally UTRPF loans personnel to normal police forces when the need arises, whether it be to assist in drug battles and corporate wars or to act as bodyguards of some particularly important UT political figure. Player characters may also find themselves involved in the pursuit of a rogue synner who has escaped to Earth—perhaps even one who turns out to be another clone of one of the PCs' donors and thus looks like an identical twin of that PC—or fighting a secret alien invasion. The PCs may even find themselves framed for something they didn't do and forced to go underground until they can clear themselves.

Colony World Adventures: Lost contact scenarios make great BUGHUNTERS™ adventures, because the PCs can do little more than guess as to what the situation will turn out to be. There are many possible reasons why contact is lost: the colony is being attacked by aliens; it has already been wiped out by an alien menace, or perhaps some unknown plague; it has revolted from UT rule; it has been taken over by a human dictator or an alien force; the equipment necessary to maintain the contact has broken down and the colonists lack the expertise or parts to fix it. In each case, the PCs have to enter the scene and discover what is wrong, without falling prey to it themselves.

Shipboard Adventures: Having a dangerous creature running loose on a starship can be incredibly frightening. But to make a good adventure of the situation, you need a fairly large ship or a creature that can hide somehow. One particularly nasty idea is to have a few small creatures that chew through stasis pods' power cables, then eat the helpless colonists within before they have a chance to wake. Alien boarding parties should be rare, so as to have make this a major event in the campaign when it does occur.

Glossary

The following terms are central to the BUGHUNTERS™ game but their meaning is not immediately obvious; thus the following brief definitions may be helpful.

AC2 ("Acey-Two")—the second planet out from Alpha Centauri; site of humanity's oldest, largest, and most successful interstellar colony

ATAPC ("a tapsy")—an **A**ll-**T**errain **A**rmored **P**ersonnel **C**arrier (armored car)

Donor—the normal human whose memories and genetic make-up are used to create a clone

E-suit—an **E**nvironmental **S**uit; a body suit which protects its wearer from hostile environments (vacuum, underwater, etc.)

Edison Point—the orbital research station at L-4

Hyperspace—the realm through which ships pass when travelling at faster-than-light speeds

Isler Drive—the hyperspace engine which makes interstellar travel practical

Isler Radio—a beam-transmitter capable of sending messages through hyperspace

L-4 and L-5—points where the Earth and Moon's gravitational fields overlap to form stable orbital points for space stations

MSO—a **M**ilitary **S**ervice **O**ccupation; a specific military profession (e.g., gunner, pilot, cook, etc.)

Ryan Shield—an electromagnetic field which screens out harmful cosmic radiation

Stasis Pod—a hybernation chamber designed to help normal humans survive hyperspace travel

Stargate—the space station at L-5 which serves as UTRPF headquarters and the launch site for interstellar journeys

Synth or Synner—a **synth**etic human or clone. All PCs in the BUGHUNTERS game are synners

Terraforming—the process of altering a planet's environment to make it more Earth-like

UT—**U**nited **T**erra; the planet-wide umbrella government responsible for running both UTRPF and its sister agency, UTSA

UTRPF ("utterpuff")—the **U**nited **T**erra **R**econnaissance and **P**eacekeeping **F**orce, the military organization entrusted with protecting Earth's colonies from hostile xenoforms. All BUGHUNTERS game PCs are members of UTRPF

UTSA—the **U**nited **T**erra **S**pace **A**ssociation; the agency responsible for coordinating spaceflight and exploration

Xenoform—alien; any lifeform which originates on a planet other than Earth

Suggested Reading and Viewing

Books

Ray Bradbury, "The City" (in *The Illustrated Man*)
John W. Campbell, "Who Goes There?"
Philip K. Dick, *Do Androids Dream of Electric Sheep?*
Joe Haldeman, *The Forever War*
Harry Harrison, *Deathworld*
Robert A. Heinlein, *Starship Trooper*, *Starman Jones*, *Tunnel in the Sky*, *The Puppet Masters*
Michael McCollum, *Antares Dawn* and *Antares Passage*
Larry Niven, "Footfall" and "The Soft Weapon"
Robert Silverberg, *The Man in the Maze*
Cordwainer Smith, "Scanners Live in Vain" and "The Game of Rat and Dragon"
John Steakly, *Armor*
James Tiptree, "The Screwfly Solution"
A. E. Van Vogt, *Voyage of the Space Beagle*
John Wyndham, *Day of the Triffids*

Video

The Abyss
Alien; *Aliens*; *Alien 3*
Blade Runner
The Blob
Critters; *Critters 2*; *Critters 3*
Dead Space
The Deep
Deep Star Six
Doctor Who: The Android Invasion; *The Planet of Evil*; *The Robots of Death*; *The Seeds of Doom*; *The Sontaran Experiment* (tv series)
Forbidden Planet
The Green Slime
The Invaders (tv series)
Invasion of the Body Snatchers
Leviathan
Outland
Predator and *Predator 2*
Runaway
Split Second
Terminator and *Terminator 2*
The Thing
V (tv series)
War of the Worlds (tv series)

Stellar Attributes and Positions

The pull-out Star Map at the end of this book and the tables on the following pages are designed to provide a quick guide to the stars near Sol. The map provides a visual reference of the position and class of all stars within 30 light years of our Solar System. The Stellar Attribute Table lists each star by position and gives a more accurate indication of its spectral class. The Stellar Distance tables list distances among all stars within 11 light years of Sol.

Stellar Map and Stellar Attribute Table

The stellar map represents a sphere centered on Sol and having a radius of 30 light years. Each star's position relative to Sol is indicated in three dimensions: X, Y, and Z. The X and Y coordinates are readily evident by the star's position on the grid; the Z coordinate is listed parenthetically after each star's name, with negative numbers indicating a position below the plane of the grid and positive numbers indicating a position above it. Note that the stars of binary and trinary systems are close enough together to warrant a single listing for the entire system.

The Stellar Attribute Table beginning in the next column lists all three coordinates for each star or system on the Star Map.

In both map and table, spectral class is given for each star and for individual stars in a binary or trinary system. On the map, the class is indicated by a color representing the star's classification; in the table, class is indicated by letter and number. The following list explains the relationship of these various items.

A: Blue (purple on map): 7,500-11,000° K

F: Blue/White (blue on map): 6,000-7,500° K

G: White/Yellow (yellow on map): 5,000-6,000° K

K: Orange/Red (orange on map): 3,500-5,000° K

M: Red (red on map): 3,500° K

d: dwarf star

D: collapsed white dwarf star

#: subclass of star

The temperatures shown indicate the average temperature for a star of that type. For example, Sol, a Type G star, is shown as yellow on the map, and its average temperature is between 5,000 to 6,000° K.

Stellar Attribute Table

Name	Class	x	y	z
36 Ophiuchi A/B/C	K0/dK1/K5	-4	-16	-8
41 Arae A/B	G8/M0	-3	-18	-19
61 Cygni A/B	K5/K7	6	-6	7
61 Ursae Majoris	G8	-24	2	17
61 Virginis	G6	-26	-9	-9
70 Ophiuchi A/B	K0/K5	0	-16	1
82 Eridani	G5	10	11	-14
AC +3°	dM2	26	12	2
AC +17°	dM4	16	-13	7
AC +18°	dM1	-2	-23	8
AC +23°	M3	-19	5	9
AC +48°	dM3	-7	-15	19
AC +65°	dM3	7	-9	24
AC +66°	M4	-11	-2	26
AC +79°	dM4	-3	0	16
AD Leonis	M4	-13	6	5
Alpha Centauri A/B	G2/dK5	-2	-1	-4
Alpha Mensae	G5	0	8	-29
Altair	A7	7	-14	2
Barnard's Star	M5	0	-6	0
BD -1°	dM2	-23	10	0
BD +2°	K7	-4	-26	1
BD +4°	K2	22	4	2
BD +6° A/B	K3/M4	17	13	2
BD +11°	M1	-25	-10	5
BD +32° A/B	dM4/M5	6	-21	14
BD +33°	K7	-8	-22	15
BD +45° A/B	M3/M3	-3	-14	15
BD +46°	dM2	-17	-8	20
BD +50°	dM0	-8	4	11
BD +53°935	M1	2	17	23

Name	Class	x	y	z	Name	Class	x	y	z
BD +53°1320/1321	M0/M0	-9	8	16	Delta Eridani	K0	17	24	-5
BD +56°	K3	12	-3	18	Delta Pavonis	G8	4	-7	-18
BD +61°	dM2	8	-8	21	DQ Pegasi A/B	M4/M6	21	-3	8
BD +63°	K0	12	6	26	Epsilon Eridani	K2	6	8	-2
BD +68°	M3	-1	-6	14	Epsilon Indi	K5	5	-3	-10
Beta Comae	G0	-23	-7	13	Eta Cassiopeiae A/B	G0/dM0	10	2	15
Beta Hydri	G2	4	0	-21	EV Lacertae	DM5	10	-4	11
Canis Minoris	dM4	-9	20	1	Fomalhaut A	A3	19	-5	-11
CC 658	DA	-6	0	-13	Fomalhaut B	K5	22	-6	-14
CD -59°	M0	-9	8	-21	Gamma Leporis A/B	F6/K5	2	25	-10
CD -51°6	M3	-17	-3	-22	Gamma Pavonis	F8	9	-8	-27
CD -51°5	K0	-18	1	-22	Groombridge 34 A/B	M1/M6	8	1	8
CD -49°	M3	8	-6	-12	Innes' Star	dM	-5	1	-8
CD -46°	M4	-2	-10	-11	Jennifer's Star	G0	-22	-3	20
CD -45°	M0	8	-12	-15	Kapteyn's Star	M0	2	9	-9
CD -44°	M5	-1	-11	-11	Keid A/B/C	K1/DA/dM4	7	14	-2
CD -44° A/B	M4/M4	-5	21	-21	Kruger 60 A/B	dM3/DM4	6	-3	11
CD -40°	M4	-9	-12	-13	Lalande	M2	-6	2	5
CD -39°	M0	7	-7	-8	Lalande 25372	M4	-14	-7	4
CD -37° A/B	M4/M7	-9	-19	-16	Lalande 46650	M2	20	-1	1
CD -36°15	M2	9	-2	-7	LFT 215	M6	18	14	11
CD -36°13 A/B	K3/M5	8	-13	-12	LFT 507	M6	-6	22	-2
CD -34° A/B/C	K3/K4/M2	-4	-19	-14	LFT 543/544	DF/M6	-8	17	-6
CD -32° A/B	dM4/dM4	15	-18	-15	LFT 598	M6	-17	21	-12
CD -31°	dM2	17	-20	-16	LFT 661	K6	-21	15	-10
CD -27°	K0	14	-21	-13	LFT 698	dM0	-26	14	-1
CD -24°	dM2	-9	-20	-10	LFT 1729	dM6	10	-4	-3
CD -21°	dM2	-1	18	-7	LFT 1747	K6	7	-2	-27
CD -21° A/B	dM2/M	13	-5	-5	LFT 1849	DA5	19	0	-18
CD -20° A/B	dK5/dM2	-13	-12	-7	Lowrey's Star	dG8	-22	1	17
CD -18°	M3	24	15	-9	Luyten 68-28/27 A/B	M/M	-7	-1	-20
CD -13°	dK0	14	17	-6	Luyten 97-12	DF	-3	6	-18
CD -12°	dM4	-5	-12	-3	Luyten 347-14	M7	4	-13	-14
CD -11°	M4	-16	-12	-4	Luyten 674-15	M6	-10	15	-7
CD -8° A/B	dM3/M4	-6	-20	-3	Luyten's Star	dM4	-4	12	1
CD -7°	dM5	-14	-16	-3	Mu Cassiopeiae	dG5	13	4	20
CD -3°	M1	3	20	-1	Mu Herculis A/B/C	G5/M4/M4	-2	-25	13
Chi Draconis	F7	1	-8	26	Orionis	F6	8	25	3
Cincinnati	dM3	12	0	-9	Piscium	K1	21	10	8
Colin's Star	dM1	6	23	-9	Procyon A/B	F5/DF	-5	10	1
Connors' Star	dM2	0	-24	-1	Proxima Centauri	M5	-2	-1	-4

Name	Class	x	y	z
Rho Eridani A/B	K2/K2	11	5	-18
Ross 41	M5	4	29	5
Ross 47	dM4	2	19	4
Ross 64	M6	-2	25	11
Ross 128	dM5	-11	1	0
Ross 154	dM4	2	-8	-4
Ross 248	dM6	7	-1	7
Ross 558	dM4	17	15	11
Ross 614 A/B	dM4/M	-2	13	-2
Ross 619	dM5	-11	18	3
Ross 730/731	dM2/dM2	7	-25	10
Ross 780	dM5	14	-4	-4
Ross 986	dM5	-4	14	12
Scirocco A/B	M3/dM4	6	-18	2
Sigma Draconis	K0	3	-6	17
Sirius A/B	A1/DA5	-2	8	-2
Sol	**G2**	**0**	**0**	**0**
Struve A/B	dM4/dM5	1	-6	10
SZ Ursae Majoris	M1	-11	2	26
Tau Ceti	G8	10	5	-3
UC 48	M6	-1	-11	-16
UV Ceti A/B	dM6/dM6	7	3	-2
Van Maanen's Star	DF3	13	3	1
Vega	A0	3	-20	17
Wolf 294	dM4	-3	16	11
Wolf 358	dM5	-22	7	3
Wolf 359	dM6	-7	2	1
Wolf 424 A/B	M7/M7	-14	-2	2
Wolf 489	DG8	-23	-10	2
Wolf 562	M6	-10	-12	-2
Wolf 629	dM4	-6	-19	-3
Wolf 922	dM4	20	-15	-4
WX Ursae Majoris A/B	M2/dM5	-13	4	13
Xi Ursae Majoris A/B	G0/G0	-23	4	14
Xi Bootis A/B	G8/dK5	-16	-14	7
Zeta Tucanae	G0	10	1	-22

Stellar Distances

No two-dimensional map can clearly indicate the actual distance between objects in three dimensions. For that reason, we include for the GM's convenience the following tables of pre-calculated stellar distances. Sol rates the longest listing because it is the most likely launching place for most BUGHUNTERS™ game missions. Following the Sol table are separate tables for each star within 11 light-years of Sol (with x, y, and z coordinates in parentheses). Each list identifies all stars within 11 light-years of that star.

With these tables, the GM is able to readily reference travel distances for the majority of probable BUGHUNTERS adventures. GMs who wish to run adventures involving the more far-flung star systems on the map—those not shown on the following tables—or to launch missions to yet more-distant stars will need to calculate the distances between them. To do so, use a calculator with square root function and the following formula:

$$D=\sqrt{[(X-x)^2 + (Y-y)^2 + (Z-z)^2]}$$

In this formula, D equals the distance between the two stars in question, the capital letters are coordinates of the star of origin, and the smaller letters those of the destination star.

For example, a GM wishing to run an adventure in which the PCs travel from Wolf 922 (position X 20, Y –15, Z –4) to Ross 619 (position x –11, y 18, z 3) would plug the numbers into the formula and solve as follows:

$$D=\sqrt{[(20 - -11)^2 + (-15 - 18)^2 + (-4 - 3)^2]}$$
$$D=\sqrt{[(31)^2 + (-33)^2 + (-7)^2]}$$
$$D=\sqrt{[961 + 1089 + 49]}$$
$$D=\sqrt{2099}$$
$$D=45.8 \text{ light years}$$

Sol
G2
(0, 0, 0)

Star	Distance
36 Ophiuchi A/B/C	18
41 Arae A/B	26
61 Cygni A/B	11
70 Ophiuchi A/B	16
82 Eridani	20
AC +17°	22
AC +23°	22
AC +48°	25
AC +79°	16
AD Leonis	15
Alpha Centauri A/B	5
Altair	16
Barnard's Star	6
BD +45° A/B	21
BD +46°	27
BD +50°	14
BD +53°1320/1321	20
BD +56°	22
BD +61°	24
BD +68°	15
Beta Hydri	21
Canis Minoris	22
CC 658	14
CD -59°	24
CD -51°6	28
CD -51°5	28
CD -49°	16
CD -46°	15
CD -45°	21
CD -44°	16
CD -44° A/B	30
CD -40°	20
CD -39°	13
CD -36°15	12
CD -36°13 A/B	19
CD -34° A/B/C	24
CD -21°	19
CD -21° A/B	15
CD -20° A/B	19

Star	Distance
CD -12°	13
CD -11°	20
CD -7°	21
CD -3°	20
Cincinnati	15
Delta Pavonis	20
Epsilon Eridani	10
Epsilon Indi	12
Eta Cassiopeiae A/B	18
EV Lacertae	15
Fomalhaut A	23
Groombridge 34 A/B	11
Innes' Star	9
Kapteyn's Star	13
Keid A/B/C	16
Kruger 60 A/B	13
Lalande	8
Lalande 25372	16
Lalande 46650	20
LFT 543/544	20
LFT 1729	11
LFT 1849	26
Luyten 68-28/27	21
Luyten 97-12	19
Luyten 347-14	20
Luyten 674-15	19
Luyten's Star	13
Mu Cassiopeiae	24
Procyon A/B	11
Rho Eridani A/B	22
Ross 47	20
Ross 128	11
Ross 154	9
Ross 248	10
Ross 614 A/B	13
Ross 619	21
Ross 780	15
Ross 986	19
Scirocco A/B	19
Sigma Draconis	18
Sirius A/B	8
Struve A/B	12
Tau Ceti	12

Star	Distance
UC 48	19
UV Ceti A/B	8
Van Maanen's Star	13
Vega	26
Wolf 294	20
Wolf 359	7
Wolf 424 A/B	14
Wolf 562	16
Wolf 629	20
WX Ursae Majoris A/B	19
Xi Bootis A/B	22

61 Cygni A/B
K5/K7
(6, -6, 7)

Star	Distance
Altair	9
Barnard's Star	9
BD +68°	10
EV Lacertae	6
Groombridge 34 A/B	7
Kruger 60 A/B	5
LFT 1729	11
Ross 248	5
Sigma Draconis	10
Sol	11
Struve A/B	6

Alpha Centauri A/B
G2/dK5
(-2, -1, -4)

Star	Distance
Barnard's Star	7
CC 658	10
CD -46°	11
CD -36°15	11
CD -12°	11
Cincinnati	11
Epsilon Indi	9

Star	Distance
Innes' Star	5
Lalande	10
Ross 128	10
Ross 154	8
Sirius A/B	9
Sol	5
UV Ceti A/B	10
Wolf 359	8

Barnard's Star
M5
(0, -6, 0)

Star	Distance
61 Cygni A/B	9
70 Ophiuchi A/B	10
Alpha Centauri A/B	7
Altair	11
CD -39°	11
CD -12°	8
Lalande	11
LFT 1729	11
Ross 154	5
Ross 248	11
Sol	6
Struve A/B	10
Wolf 359	11

Epsilon Eridani
K2
(6, 8, -2)

Star	Distance
Kapteyn's Star	8
Keid A/B/C	6
Luyten's Star	11
Ross 614 A/B	9
Sirius A/B	8
Sol	10
Tau Ceti	5
UV Ceti A/B	5
Van Maanen's Star	9

Groombridge 34 A/B
M1/M6
(8, 1, 8)

Star	Distance
61 Cygni A/B	7
BD +56°	11
Eta Cassiopeiae A/B	7
EV Lacertae	6
Kruger 60 A/B	5
Ross 248	2
Sol	11
Struve A/B	10
UV Ceti A/B	10
Van Maanen's Star	9

Innes' Star
dM
(-5, 1, -8)

Star	Distance
Alpha Centauri A/B	5
CC 658	5
Cincinnati	7
Epsilon Indi	11
Kapteyn's Star	11
Luyten 97-12	11
Ross 128	10
Sirius A/B	10
Sol	9
Wolf 359	9

Lalande
M2
(-6, 2, 5)

Star	Distance
AD Leonis	8
Alpha Centauri A/B	10
Barnard's Star	11
BD +50°	7
Luyten's Star	11

Star	Distance
Procyon A/B	9
Ross 128	7
Sirius A/B	10
Sol	8
Wolf 359	4
Wolf 424 A/B	9
WX Ursae Majoris A/B	11

LFT 1729
dM6
(10, -4, -3)

Star	Distance
61 Cygni A/B	11
Barnard's Star	11
CD -49°	9
CD -39°	7
CD -36°15	5
CD -21° A/B	4
Epsilon Indi	9
Lalande 46650	11
Ross 154	9
Ross 248	11
Ross 780	4
Sol	11
Tau Ceti	9
UV Ceti A/B	8
Van Maanen's Star	9

Procyon A/B
F5/DF
(-5, 10, 1)

Star	Distance
AD Leonis	10
Canis Minoris	11
Lalande	9
LFT 543/544	10
Luyten 674-15	11
Luyten's Star	2
Ross 128	11

Star	Distance
Ross 614 A/B	5
Ross 619	10
Sirius A/B	5
Sol	11
Wolf 359	8

Ross 128
dM5
(-11, 1, 0)

Star	Distance
AD Leonis	7
Alpha Centauri A/B	10
Cincinnati	9
Innes' Star	10
Lalande	7
Lalande 25372	9
Procyon A/B	11
Sol	11
Wolf 359	4
Wolf 424 A/B	5

Ross 154
dM4
(2, -8, -4)

Star	Distance
36 Ophiuchi A/B/C	11
70 Ophiuchi A/B	10
Alpha Centauri A/B	8
Altair	10
Barnard's Star	5
CD -49°	10
CD -46°	8
CD -44°	8
CD -39°	6
CD -36°15	10
CD -36°13 A/B	11
CD -21° A/B	11
CD -12°	8
Epsilon Indi	8

Star	Distance
LFT 1729	9
Luyten 347-14	11
Scirocco A/B	12
Sol	9

Ross 248
dM6
(7, -1, 7)

Star	Distance
61 Cygni A/B	5
Barnard's Star	11
Eta Cassiopeiae A/B	9
EV Lacertae	6
Groombridge 34 A/B	2
Kruger 60 A/B	5
LFT 1729	11
Sol	10
Struve A/B	8
UV Ceti A/B	10
Van Maanen's Star	9

Sirius A/B
A1/DA5
(-2, 8, -2)

Star	Distance
Alpha Centauri A/B	9
CD -21°	11
Epsilon Eridani	8
Innes' Star	10
Kapteyn's Star	8
Keid A/B/C	11
Lalande	10
Luyten's Star	5
Procyon A/B	5
Ross 614 A/B	5
Sol	8
UV Ceti A/B	10
Wolf 359	8

UV Ceti A/B
dM6/dM6
(7, 3, -2)

Star	Distance
Alpha Centauri A/B	10
CD -36°15	7
CD -21° A/B	10
Epsilon Eridani	5
Epsilon Indi	10
Groombridge 34 A/B	10
Kapteyn's Star	10
Keid A/B/C	11
LFT 1729	8
Ross 248	10
Ross 780	10
Sirius A/B	10
Sol	8
Tau Ceti	4
Van Maanen's Star	7

Wolf 359
dM6
(-7, 2, 1)

Star	Distance
AD Leonis	8
Alpha Centauri A/B	8
Barnard's Star	11
BD +50°	10
Cincinnati	11
Innes' Star	9
Lalande	4
Luyten's Star	10
Procyon A/B	8
Ross 128	4
Sirius A/B	8
Sol	7
Wolf 424 A/B	8

BUGHUNTERS™ Player-Character Record Sheet

Background Information

Character Name: _____ Date Created: _____ Experience Points: _____

MSO: _____ Player: _____ Temp. Ex. Pts.: _____

Rank: _____ Donor Background: _____

Rank Points/Income: _____ Donor Condition: _____

Savings: _____

Attributes

Physique Dice: _____ Intellect Dice: _____ Spirit Dice: _____ Influence Dice: _____

Fitness: _____ Learning: _____ Psyche: _____ Charm: _____

Reflexes: _____ Intuition: _____ Willpower: _____ Position: _____

Stamina Points: _____ Body Points: _____

Skills

(Learning skills are italicized, as a reminder that they may not be used unless possessed.)
BASIC TRAINING: First Aid (Medicine pool), Small Arms (Firearms pool), Unarmed Combat (Physical Disciplines pool)

COMPUTER
__Computer Systems (Int)
  __*Comp. Prog. (Lea)*

COVERT ACTIONS
__Camouflage (Int)
__Disguise (Cha)
__Lockpick, Mech. (Ref)
__Searching (Int)
__*Security Systems (Lea)*
  __*Lockpick, Elec. (Lea)*
__Stealth (Ref)
__*Survival (Lea)*

ENGINEERING
__Engin., Electrical (Int)
  __*Electronic (Lea)*
    __*Computer (Lea)*
    __*Isler Drive (Lea)*
    __*Stasis Field (Lea)*
__Engin., Mechanical (Int)
  __*Firearm (Lea)*
  __*Power Plant (Lea)*
    __*Nuclear (Lea)*
  __*Vehicle (Lea)*
    __*Aircraft (Lea)*
    __*Spacecraft (Lea)*
    __*Surf. craft (Lea)*
__*Engin., Environ. (Lea)*

FIREARMS
__Small Arms (Ref)
  __Sidearms (Ref)
  _____
  __Longarms (Ref)
  _____
  _____
__Heavy Weap. (Ref)
  __Anti-Armor (Fit)
  __Gr. Launch. (Fit)
  __Mortars (Int)
  __Autofire (Fit)

HUMANITIES
__Art (Int)
__Bureaucracy (Int)
__Cooking (Int)
__*History (Lea)*
__*Law (Lea)*
__*Linguistics (Lea)*
__Literature (Int)
  __Writing (Cha)
__Music (Int)
  __Instrument (Cha)
__*Philosophy (Lea)*
__Protocol (Int)
__*Religion (Lea)*
__*Sports (Lea)*
__Xeno. Theory (Int)

LANGUAGES (Int)
  _____

MEDICINE
__First Aid (Int)
__*General Med. (Lea)*
  __*Emergen. Med. (Lea)*
  __*Psychiatry (Lea)*
  __*Stasis Med. (Lea)*
  __*Surgery (Lea)*
  __*Synthetic Med. (Lea)*

MILITARY
__Comm Gear (Int)
  __*Comm Proc. (Lea)*
  __*Isler Radio (Lea)*
__*Demolitions (Lea)*
__E-Suit (Int)
__Gunnery (Int)
__Leadership (Cha)
__*Military Science (Lea)*

PERSONALITY
__Bluffing (Cha)
  __Bargaining (Cha)
  __Gambling (Cha)
__Luck (Psy)
__Street Smarts (Cha)
__Trivia (Wil)

PHYSICAL DISCIPLINES
__Armed Combat (Ref)
  _____
__Athletics (Ref)
__Brawling (Fit)
__Climbing (Ref)
__Grappling (Ref)
__High-G Maneuver (Fit)
__Low-G Maneuver (Ref)
__Swimming (Fit)
__Throwing (Ref)

__Unarmed Combat (Ref)
  _____

SCIENCES
__General Sciences (Int)
  __*Biology (Lea)*
  __*Chemistry (Lea)*
  __*Physics (Lea)*
  __*Psychology (Lea)*

TRAVEL
__Nav., Planetary (Int)
  __*Space (Lea)*
    __*Hyper. (Lea)*
__Piloting, Surface (Int)
  __*Aerospace (Lea)*
    __*Hyper. (Lea)*

Weapons

Type	Weight	Mag.	ROF	Damage	Range	Skill	Recoil Mod.
1. ____	____	____	____	____	____	____	____
2. ____	____	____	____	____	____	____	____
3. ____	____	____	____	____	____	____	____
4. ____	____	____	____	____	____	____	____

Equipment Table

Ranged Attacks

Type	Mag.	ROF	Damage	Range	Skill
Rock	—	1	1d3(2)	thrown	Throwing
Knife	—	1	1d4(3)	thrown	Throwing
Axe	—	1	1d8(3)	thrown	Throwing
Spear	—	1	1d10(3)	thrown	Throwing
Pistol, Stun	13	3		15/30/50	Sidearms
Small setting			1d10(0)		
Human setting			2d10(1)		
Large setting			4d10(2)		
Pistol, Small	4	4	1d6(3)	10/20/40	Sidearms
Pistol, Large		3			Sidearms
Standard	13		1d8(4)	20/35/50	
JA	10		2d10(5)	25/50/90	
Pistol, Heavy		3			Sidearms
Standard/Tracer	13		1d10(4)	20/40/60	
Splatter	12		2d10(7)	20/40/60	
HEJA	7		3d10(7)	30/60/100	
Machine Pistol	150	5/x12/150	1d6(3)	30/80/150	Sidearms/Autofire
Rifle, Civilian	6	2	1d8(5)	50/150/300	Longarms
Rifle, Tranquilizer	30	5	tranquilizes*	40/100/200	Longarms
Rifle, Assault	200	5/x8/25	1d12(6)	50/150/250	Longarms/Autofire
Shotgun, Civilian	1-5	2	2d6(5)	10/50/80	Longarms
Shotgun, Special Forces	15	1/x4/12	see next entry	15/60/90	Longarms/Autofire
Shotgun, Automatic	30	1/x8/15		20/60/90	Longarms/Autofire
Flechette			2d6(7)		
Explosive			3d8(8)		
AP			2d10(9)		
Grenade Launcher	15	1	see grenades		Grenade Launcher
Direct				100/200/300	
Indirect				400	
Flechette			2d8(7)	25/70/100	
Mortar, Small	—	2	see grenades	400	Mortars
Flame Thrower	10	1/x5/10	2d6(4)/turn	5/10/15	Heavy Weap./Autofire
Machine Gun, Howler	2000	4/x50/500			Heavy Weap./Autofire
Standard/Tracer			1d10(4)	25/50/80	
Splatter			2d10(7)	25/50/80	
HEJA			3d10(7)	35/70/100	
HEAP			3d12(8)	25/50/80	
HEAT			4d10(9)	25/50/80	
UHDUG			4d12(9)	25/50/80	
Laser, Sniper	10	2	3d10(6)	100/250/400	Heavy Weapons
Laser, Repeating	5000	2/x6/100	4d10(6)	200/500/1000	Gunnery
Missile Launcher	10	1	20d10(9)**	200/500/2000	Heavy Weapons

Equipment Table

Explosive Attacks

Type	Damage
Smoke Grenade	obscures vision
Stun Grenade	16/—/—
Frag Grenade	16/80%/4d10(4)
Incendiary Grenade	16/90%/2d12(4)***
HE Mortar Round	24/90%/4d12(4)
Satchel Charge	
Shapeless	80/70%/10d10(8)
Shaped, front	200/90%/20d10(9)
Shaped, sides & rear	60/40%/5d10(5)

Hand-to-Hand Attacks

Type	Init. Mod.	Damage
Hand	0	1d4(1)
Foot	–1	1d6(1)
Club	0	1d8(2)
Knife	0	1d6(3)
Machete/Axe	–2	1d8(5)
Spear/Fixed Bayonet	–2	1d6(4)

Other Damages****

Type	Damage
Tackle	1d10(1)
Falling	1d6/2 m
Fire, normal	1d6/turn
Fire, intense	2d6/turn
Vacuum	1d12/turn

   * Unconscious for 1-5 hours.
  ** Plus side/rear effects of satchel charge.
 *** (—/—/per turn)
**** The GM should assign lethality ratings to these as desired.

Index of Tables

Combat System Summary

This page summarizes important combat rules for easy reference. Modifiers for computer sights, recoil, etc. should be noted on individual character sheets, as needed.

Skill Modifiers

Situation	Modifier
Unknown skill	½ chance
Unknown specialty	–20
Enhancement	+10
Target vital spot	½ chance
Target non-vital spot	⅒ chance

Combat Movement Rates (Normal G)

Type	Distance in meters/turn
Walk	15
Run	Fit
Sprint	Fit x2 (⅒ Fit duration)

Encumbrance (Normal G)

Load (kg)	Combat Effect
Fit	None
Fit x2	½ run or sprint
Fit x3	No run or sprint

Combat Round Sequence

I. Roll for Advantage* (1st round only)
II. Decide Actions
III. Determine Initiative
IV. Resolve Actions

*A side with advantage goes first and gains a +5 bonus to attack actions, etc.; the other side goes second and suffers a –5 penalty to such actions.

Advantage Modifiers*

Ambusher	+10 F9
Ambushee	–10 F8

*Failure margin is the chance of being surprised. A surprised side does nothing for one round while its opponents receive a +5 bonus to attack actions, etc. The opponents also automatically receive a subsequent round of advantage (see footnote above for effects).

Initiative

1d10 plus ⅒th of Reflexes score(s)

Actions Possible by Movement Type

Stationary: Any action
Walk: Any action but aimed fire
Run: Any hand-to-hand action, autofire, burst, or throw
Sprint: No action but tackle

Special Maneuvers

Stand: Rise from prone or kneeling
Kneel: +5 to ranged fire; possible cover
Leap: See page 51

Hand-to-Hand Actions

Tackle: Ref vs. Ref; 1d10 damage and/or pin
Grapple: Grapple skill; Fit vs. Fit to escape; see page 48
Strike: Armed Combat, Unarmed Combat, or Brawling skill; damage by weapon type

Ranged Fire Actions

Throwing: Throwing skill; throw 1 kg ½ Fit in meters
Aimed Fire: Appropriate Firearms skill; one shot at +15
Snapfire: Appropriate Firearms skill; multiple shots (weapon ROF) at no modifier
Burst Fire: Appropriate Firearms skill; –10 walking/–30 running; x2 damage, +1 lethality
Autofire: Autofire skill; –30 per 45° arc; x4 damage, +3 lethality; hinders movement
Indirect Fire: Indirect Fire or FO Comm Procedure skill; see page 50

Fire Ranges

Range: Unaided/with Visor or Scope

Sighting: 50 m specific target area/ 150 m same
Point-Blank: +10 to hit/ +20 to hit
Short: Unmodified/ +5 to hit
Medium: –5 to hit/ Unmodified
Long: –15 to hit/ –5 to hit
Extreme: –30 to hit/ –15 to hit